Stop Arguing With Me

Stop Arguing With Me

Healing an Argumentative Spirit

Dr. Duane Cuthbertson

Baal Hamon Publishers

Akure   London   New York

ISBN 10: 9784956578

ISBN 13: 978-9784956574

International Correspondence:
Baal Hamon,
27 Old Gloucester Street,
London,
WC1N 3AX,
England.

www.baalhamonpublishers.com
publishers@baalhamon.com

Dedicated to my bride of many years, Marilyn.

Thank you for your patience.

Contents

Introduction

The words from the book "jumped" at me. "Each of our lives is a narrative..." Did you catch it? Our life has a story line.

It gets profound. Psalms 139: 13 – 16 states that God, "...made all the delicate, inner parts of my body, and knit them together in my mother's womb. Thank You for making me so wonderfully complex! It is amazing to think about. Your workmanship is marvelous – and how will I know it. You were there while I was being formed in utter seclusion! You saw me before I was born and scheduled each day of my life before I began to breathe. Every day was recorded in your Book" (The Living Bible). God created you. It is sobering, but He meant for you to have that nose, those ears, and yes - those feet. God affirmed His standard for beauty through you. You are one of a kind. And He not only "saw us before we were born", he "scheduled each day of our lives before we began to breathe".

Stop Arguing With Me

Our struggles have been a part of God's processing in our lives, and He has brought us to this very point to reshape us. After reading this, you will never need to argue again.

Hopefully, the sharing of my struggles with anger will help you. This is my "story" but your interest in the book relates that perhaps it is your story "too".

Porkchop's story is different. I first met Porkchop while teaching at the East Tennessee Penitentiary. His mother had died when he was young. His father raised him, and he was the oldest of four boys. His father was seldom home, and Porkchop was placed in authority over the other children. His father would say. "If your brothers give you any trouble, beat the ____ out of them". And he did – he became angry and aggressive. In time, Bill (real name) was confronted in a bar, and during a fight, he killed a man. In prison, other inmates knew not to "mess with" Porkchop. It was known that he had a temper (he killed another man while in prison). To the best of my knowledge, Porkchop is now out of prison, but he paid dearly for his anger with many, many years of incarceration.

But I had to understand. It is the way that God put me together. Ephesians 1: 17 -18 states, "That the God of our Lord Jesus Christ, the Father of Glory, may give unto you the spirit of wisdom and revelation in the knowledge of Him. The eyes of your understanding being enlightened . . . " How would you like to have God give to you the spirit of wisdom and revelation? How would you like to have the "eyes of your understanding enlightened? By God's grace, that potential is there".

After a couple foundational chapters, we will defend our premise that the argumentative spirit can be healed. We will defend it as a sickness, but we will affirm the hope that a healing can ensue. All we ask of you is a willingness to change....to become an entirely different person.

1

Biblical Anthropology

It is true that there is "nothing new under the sun". The feelings and apprehensions of most tensions and struggles historically have always been there. The challenge of scientific inquiry is to define, and explore, and categorize. We will be crystallizing this in our studying of the etiology of an argumentative spirit.

We call anthropology the "study of man"; and we call physiology the "study of normal functions of living things or their organs". Psychology became the "study of human behavior and mental functions", and sociology the "study of human society and culture". Do you sense with me, the quest of science for understanding and preciseness? I wonder who initially created these terms, and I wonder how long it took for these studies to assume credibility.

My assumption is simple - something has been missing in this study of man.

1

Why do we have so much stress in our lives? Why can this stress have different manifestations? Why do some people have alcohol problems while some do not? Some people struggle with drugs. To other individuals, drugs are not a factor in their lives. And yes - people struggle with an argumentative spirit in different ways.

Let's call it Stress Anthropology. Stress Anthropology is the "science of diagnosing and assessing the etiology (source) of the tensions in man". Does the expression not connote a source? Tension always says something. For those of you reading this material who are counsellors, is it not imperative that you are able to identify the etiology (source) of the struggles in your patients?

Let's consider some presuppositions:

1) **Struggles manifest interpretative energy.** When we interpret the actions of people who are struggling, we not only interpret the external manifestation (depressed, angry etc), but we are also interpreting the "energy". We might conclude: "Why are they so quiet? Why are they so angry?" If we consider momentarily that awesome passage about the tongue in James 3 verse 10 that relates that "out of the same mouth proceedeth blessing and cursing...." Now, praise the Lord. We have never had "blessings and curses" both come from our mouths. Right? As the father of five children, and at last count eighteen grandchildren, it has always been my contention that the best stress

2

takes place on the way to church. "Hurry up, sit down, leave your sister alone . . ." And we walk into the sanctuary, and relate, "hi brother, hi sister . . ." I am sure on occasions my children thought, "who are these people?"

2) **Struggles are universal.** During my adolescence, I had a friend whose mother was deaf mute. They communicated in "sign language". When they argued, their fingers would fly. I used to relate to him that perhaps the world would be better if we all had to communicate in "sign language" rather than with our tongues. What would you feel if you were in the market when a terrorist bomb exploded and you witnessed death around you? And imagine people like Bin Laden "training" people to be terrorists. They were trained to hate, to be enraged, to be angry, to destroy, and to kill. We can only conjecture the feelings of the terrorist pilots on September 11, 2001 as the planes were about to hit the World Trade Center. Were they sick? Yes. Let me be presumptuous. The struggles are universal, and the solution can be universal. If this book has credibility, then anger potentially can be universally modified. The material is not only for international terrorists; it is for you. What do you feel toward your neighbor, your boss, your extended family? Can those feelings go away?

We are all caught in this "human dilemma". We have a "powerful force within us that is striving to destroy us and to lead us into unrighteousness." Sigmond Freud called it the "id" and the Bible calls it "sin". Whether we approach this material as a "religious believer" or as a skeptic, we all can relate to our capacity to be dishonest, immoral, and disillusioned. Theologian Lewis Berkhof defined sin as "essentially a breaking away from God, opposition to God and transgression of the laws of God . . ." David after his sin with Bathseba in Psalm 51: 1 – 3, related that "against thee only have I sinned and done this evil in thy sight. Blot out my transgressions, wash me thoroughly from mine iniquity, and cleanse me from my sins". I am not suggesting that this is all inclusive, but a study of the Hebrew language relates from this passage that our sin nature has at least three parts. The word "transgression" means that we are in a state of rebellion. The word "iniquity" implies that the bent of our lives is away from God. And the word "sin" connotes that we have all missed the mark. We all fall short of God's standard of holiness and righteousness. Now praise the Lord   . . . you have never been intentionally rebellious? Amen. And praise the Lord, you have never done something deliberately wrong? I have contended that the strongest evidence for our "sin nature" is that we know something is wrong, and we still decide to do it.

Conversely, we have a "good nature". Genesis 1: 26 – 27 states that man was created in the "image of God". Without elaborate defense, God placed His imprint within us. We all have a "God-like-ness" quality. Words and

4

expressions such as conscience, guilt, and altruism come from this quality. Sociologically, this has led to values, and moral, and ethics.

Do these two "parts" of us ever come into conflict? Oh . . . about all the time. It is the "human dilemma". What do you feel when your children talk back? What do you feel when your wife wants you to go shopping? What do you feel when someone cuts in front of you in the store? Note how the good and the bad natures create tension. I recall in counseling a dentist. I inquired, "What is your response when people do not pay their bills." He said, "Well, I get up in the middle of the night, and throw a rock through one of their windows." He continued, "But I am fair. If it is a little bill, I take out a small window, and if it is a big bill, I take out the front window."

While teaching at East Tennessee Penitentiary, I noted that a man was sitting away from the others in class. I started talking to him. He immediately stopped me, and explained, "You don't want to talk to me. If you talk to me, the others will not talk to you." "Why," I inquired. He continued, "There is an unwritten law in this prison that if you violate a child, you are ostracized by the population...kill a policeman and you are a hero. Violate a child and you are ostracized." He was a pedophile. I eventually successfully addressed this in class. Even in prison there were "unwritten" laws of perceived goodness.

3) **It starts before birth.** God has placed within the child a particular "bent" or temperament (Psalm 139). Temperament is our behavioral style. It is the "how" rather than the "what" or the "why". Technically, it can be defined as "the characteristic tempo, rhythmicity, adaptability, energy expenditure, mood, and focus of attention of the child, independently of the content of any specific behavior". Temperament is not interchangeable. Like any other characteristic of an organism, its features can develop and be significantly affected by environmental circumstances. Few adults are aware of how the nature-nurture interplay has affected them; they do not stop to think. Was I a defiant youngster? Is there a correlation between that and my aggressiveness in business? Was I a sensitive child, and is that why I still have difficulty meeting people?

Doctors Alexander Thomas, Stella Chess, and Herbet Birch once studied the temperaments of 141 children from thirty-five families over a period of ten years. They summarized their conclusions in their excellent book, Temperament and Behaviour Disorders in Children (New York University Press). They recognized that temperament cannot be the "heart and body of general theory" but felt that "we must give as much attention to temperament as environment."

Chess, Birch, and Thomas concluded that a child has genetic predispositions in nine areas: activity, rhythmicity, approach or withdrawal, adaptability, intensity of reaction, threshold of responsiveness, quality of mood, distractibility, and attention span and persistence. One researcher suggested that there could be 4,500 variables. There could be 4,500 differences of mood, etc.

Chess, Birch, and Thomas identified three different temperaments – the easy child, the slow-to-warm-up child, and the difficult child. In my studies, I proposed four categories: (1) the defiant child, (2) the irritable child, (3) the sensitive child, and (4) the compliant child.

Let's briefly categorize each of these: (1) The defiant child acts out his feelings, usually responds negatively to new stimuli, is constantly striking out to others, and his mood is usually negative and his reactions are intense. (2) The irritable child is determined to get their own way, has a strong desire to get what they want, is generally a very active person, and usually harder to lead. (3) The sensitive child demands much attention and affection, in new situation usually withdraws at first and adapts slowly, slow to accept new people, and can easily develop feelings of depression and loneliness. (4) The compliant child is generally positive in mood, the intensity of his reaction are generally low or mild, is rapidly adaptable, and generally evokes pleasant responses in other people. Would you categorize yourself as being defiant, irritable, sensitive, or compliant? (You might refer to my book, *Raising Your Child, Not Your Voice* for further information).

Stop Arguing With Me

Many years ago, I was privileged to escort some 300 teenagers on a vacation trip to England. It was such a delight to explore this picturesque and historical country. We all fell in love with our witty and verbose "cockney" guide. One day during a personal discussion of Princess Anne and Prince Charles, he concluded his comments with a pointed, rhetorical question, "Duane, would you have been any different if you were born Prince Charles (next King of England)?" My response might shock you. I retorted, "You know, I think I could have done it; in due respect, I don't believe that Prince Charles is any smarter than I am. He just had different parents. It does make a difference who your parents are." It is conjecture, but would you have been different if you were born say Chelsea Clinton or Franklin Graham?

Without question, the temperament of a child "interacts" with the environment. In correlating environment to temperament studies relate:

(1) A "negative" child may be more positive if experiences are gentle and favorable, (2) a very adaptable child may become hardened in a hostile home, and (3) a difficult child can become intolerable with excessive discipline. Conversely, in correlating temperament to environment: (1) the ease of difficulty in caring for the child can be a factor, (2) the degree of congeniality of the child's temperament can be a factor, and (3) the congruence of parental expectation with child can be a factor.

Thus, when a child is under stress and tension by his environment, there will be avarice in each child both in response and effect. Pressure can lead to motivation and performance in one, or conversely, pressure can lead to frustration and ineptness in another. The "make-up" of the individual becomes the deviation.

Below is the "Cuthbertson Environmental-Stress" Inventory. Scale all the tables from one through ten. Place that number (between one and ten) that would be most consistent with your home pattern. Add up the numbers and place the total at the bottom. Check the total with the chart for correlation.

Place the number

CUTHBERTSON CHILD STRESS INVENTORY

The purpose of this inventory is to measure the pressure that parents place on their children. Obviously, there is a variant amount among children both in response and effect. Pressure can lead to motivation and performance, or conversely, pressure can lead to frustration and ineptness. The make-up of the individual child becomes the deviation.

Scale all six tables from one through ten. Place that number (between one and ten) that would be most consistent with your home pattern. Add up the numbers and place the total at the bottom. Check the total with the chart for correlation.

FACTOR	DEFINITION AND SCALE	YOUR SCORE
Security Much Love & Affection	Meeting emotional needs of child 1---------5----------10	Little love & affection
STRETCHING Push child little	Your expectation of the child 1---------5----------10	Push child much
STRESSES Little social pressure	Pressure on child outside home 1---------5----------10	Much social pressure
SHUFFLING Moved Little	Mobility, how much moving 1---------5----------10	Moved much
STRUGGLES Little home tension	Conflict between parents 1---------5----------10	Much home tension
SHAPING Consistent example	Consistency of your lifestyle 1---------5----------10	Inconsistent example
	CHART CORRELATION:	TOTAL _____
44 – 60	Unreasonable stress and motivation on child	
30 – 45	Above Average stress and motivation on child	
18 – 29	Average stress and motivation on child	
0 – 17	Motivation needed on child	

4) **Struggles connote the potential for perfection and wholeness.** I have a cartoon of two ministers commenting on a new signboard in front of one of the churches. Across the signboard is the title for the next Sunday sermon. The topic is "Thou shalt not covet thy neighbor's goods." One of the ministers asks, "How do you like it (the new signboard)?" The other minister comments, "very nice. . ." But then after some reflection he continues, "but I wish we had a signboard like that at our church." I love it. Our society thrives on a context of excellence. We pay professional athletes millions . . . that's millions of dollars . . . to play adolescent's games. We give A's, and B's, and F's for grades in our schools. Don't you love the bumper sticker, "My son/daughter is an honor student at such and such . . ." Why?

David Myers, in his book *Social Psychology*, defines self-serving bias as "the tendency to perceive oneself favorably." Perception is everything. There is reality as it is and reality as we perceive it. When two individuals perceive reality differently, there is always the potential for tension. Psychologically, this is called cognitive dissonance, defined as being "feelings of tension that arise when one is simultaneously aware of two inconsistent cognitions". Said more simply, many couples think "my spouse would be better if he/she were more like me". I contend that in the vast majority of marriages, the assumption is that we will change our spouse. Consciously and subconsciously, for some, this leads to a "oneness" in the relationship. For others, they "argue" for fifty years over the same, that's same, issues. The "oneness" never happens. I know it is hard to believe but there are people who argue more than once over the same issue.

Any tension . . . any attempt through argumentation to change other's opinions connotes an ideal. Rationally and intuitively, you believe you are correct. Why?

Let's explore three arguments for this perfection:

A Biblical Defense: In the Bible, Matthew 5: 48 states "Be ye perfect as your Father in Heaven is perfect." The Greek word for perfect connotes "being a full age, mature, complete." The same God, who saw me in my mother's womb, before I was born (Psalm 139), is the same God who called me before the "foundations of the world" (1 Timothy 1: 9). It is the same God who from the offset of my salvation and through my life sees me "whole and complete". Ephesians 4: 12 sets forth a three-fold purpose of the Church: (1) the work of the ministry, (2) the edifying of the body (the church), and (3) the "perfecting" of the saints. Here, it states that it is through the Church that I have the potential of becoming "fully equipped" to become the person that God desires to develop. Generally, the church could do better in understanding and developing the "perfect" (complete) saint and in fairness to the church, perhaps the leadership and resources are not available. This concept in practice would involve isolating and developing each person within the church, and helping them to recognize their spiritual gifts, putting them to work within the body, and helping them to be equipped.

There is an anti-thesis. Many years ago while involved in Christian radio, I created and produced a daily interview program. In one of the interviews, a guest was expounding on a verse in John 10: 10. It states, "The thief comes to steal, to kill, and destroy . . . but I come that ye might have life and have it more abundantly." The lady commented, "The devil here is giving us his game plan." She continued. "The first thing that he does is steal our joy, then he kills our spirit (the depression and frustration), and finally, he destroys our soul and body." I am aware that this is conjecture, but the profoundness hit me immediately. Most of us have been unhappy at some time in our life. I retorted, "There are two ramifications that hit me immediately: (1) I am never going to be unhappy another day of my life and (2) Everything that is negative comes from Hell itself (as I stated it then). So the boundaries are set. God is striving to move us toward "completeness" and the devil is striving to "destroy" us.

I trust that you understand that this "completeness" is not "sinless perfection". It connotes the reaching of our full potential. I believe it to be synonymous with theorists such as Abraham Maslow and Carl Jung as they discussed "self actualization" and "individuation".

A Pragmatic Defense: As I have already implied, this is a sociological defense. I call it intimidation by perfection. As I previously alluded, society has created a context of excellence. As of this writing, a star athlete for the Detroit Tigers baseball team is signing a contract for some seven million dollars a year. Now considering his physical size, I am gambling that he will never read this book. I contend that no athlete is worth $7,000,000 annually. The President of the United States makes some $400,000 yearly. How did we create a society where an athlete makes overwhelmingly more money than the president? The "perfection" is intuitive. We are all experts on raising the neighbor's kids and we do have opinions about everything. This context of "intuitive perfection" has permeated the socialization process. Some people are more "religious" than others. Some people are "better-looking" than others. The etiology of "perfection" must come from within man himself. Scripturally, as early as Genesis, chapter four, Cain was "jealous" of his brother Abel. He became angry and killed him.

The Philosophical Defense: I was in a philosophy class in college and the professor had just related that Socrates believed "that everything was relative, but if everything was relative then there had to be an absolute." He continued as he wandered around class and touched a desk. "This is not really a chair, it is a symbol of a chair, but the fact that we call it a chair means somewhere at least conceptually, there has to be an ideal chair. . .". The class then enjoyed verbally the process of creating that ideal chair with its soft cushions, built-in refrigerator, etc. . .

But I was not ready for his next scenario. He continued his walk in the classroom, and he began putting his hands on the shoulders of various students. He commented, "This is not really a Davis. This is a symbol of a Davis, but somewhere out there is an ideal Davis. This is not really a Cuthbertson. This is a symbol of a Cuthbertson, but somewhere out there is an ideal Cuthbertson." (Put in your own name). This is not really a _____. And somewhere out there is an ideal _____. Theologically, sociologically, and philosophically an "ideal" us is attainable. And our response to each of our struggles connotes whether we are advancing or declining. Many, however, have neither the perception nor insight to understand. So we argue and argue and argue again. Before we can understand the dysfunctional, we must understand the functional. If we know what has broken down, we can better understand how to fix it. So hold on tight, the argumentative spirit can be healed.

2

Psychophysical Unity

Our quest is to find the source. It has been my delight to teach "Abnormal Psychology" at various Christian colleges. As I related to the students, your intervention with others will be limited if you can't diagnose the problem. This chapter will lay foundation in understanding the "structure of man."

Maybe I am presumptuous. Forgive me. I am aware that our church fathers have debated this issue from the second century. Is man dichotomous (two parts: spiritual and physical) or is he trichotomous (three parts: spirit, soul, and body)? David Myers and Malcolm Jeeves in their book, *Psychology Through the Eyes of Faith* defend what they call a "psychophysical unity." Using philosophy and defense from the Old and New Testaments, they defend that Biblical passages emphasize wholeness. "The details of Hebrew psychology differ from the details of contemporary science, but one fundamental point on which they both agree: mind and emotions are inextricably linked with the body. The people of the Old Testament thought with their hearts, felt with their bowels, and their flesh longed for God. Of the body organs, the heart was the most important. In the 851 Old Testament uses of heart, it continually denotes the whole personality . . ." Of course, we exist as a whole person. But does not that infer that the whole will be influenced by its parts? Now we must ask if there is enough Biblical distinction to divide the spirit and the soul? I contend that the strongest argument for the former is that in Scripture, and I am aware that this not all-inclusive, we have three different words used for the structure of man. We also have scriptures that refer to three "differential" parts within this same context. Church Father Origen strongly accepted and defended this trichotomous conclusion as being consistent with Scripture. Origen even took the words *soma* (body), *psyche* (soul) and *pneuma* (spirit) as clues to the proper method of interpreting all Scripture. I believe that the church is indebted to him for his insight. I will utilize this structure throughout this material.

In the creation of man, Genesis 2: 7 relates, "And the Lord God formed man out of the dust of the ground, and breathed into his nostrils the breath of life; and man became a living soul." Note that Adam was made from the dust of the earth (body), and God breathed into him the breath of life (spirit), and he became a living soul (soul). Hebrew 4: 12 comments on the power of the Word of God, how it can "pierce asunder . . . dividing soul and spirit, and of the joints and marrow (body) . . ." Notice in both of these passages is the assumption of man having three parts.

The strongest Biblical passage in this defense in found in 1 Thessalonians 5:23. "And the very God of peace sanctify you wholly, and I pray God that your whole spirit, soul, and body be preserved blameless unto the coming of our Lord Jesus Christ". Notice that the context of "perfection and completeness" is not only emphasized in the "structural analysis," but God is so determined that we don't miss the point, that He emphasizes the concept of wholeness twice in the passage. "Sanctify you *wholly* (completely) . . . that you *whole* spirit, soul, and body . . ."

W. E. Ward, in the *Evangelical Dictionary of Theology*, states that "the present theological and psychological emphasis is based almost altogether upon the fundamental wholeness or unity of man's being and against all philosophical attempts to divide him." That's . . . "being against all philosophical attempts to divide him. Our evangelical seminaries teach hermeneutically to exegete Biblically from the smallest to the largest, and even the Scriptures state that every "jot and tittle" (smallest parts of the Hebrew language in Holy Writ) is inspired. Yet, we still have avoided the challenge of applying these same principles psychologically. Gestalt psychology views man as a whole. The Reductionists start with the smallest parts and build to the whole. Philosophically, that will be our approach in this material.

We have established the premise that God wants us to be whole and complete. Does that not presuppose that the "wholeness" must have parts? And for the sake of argument, if the "wholeness" has the potential for completeness, can there be completeness in each of the parts? And psychologically when something "breaks down," what part is breaking down? What then is the origin of an argumentative spirit? How is it fed?

Let's establish some presumptions before we divulge the structure.

(1)   **This interpretative energy can be defined.** If I cut myself, I bleed. If I choose to run my car into a tree, there will be devastating results. Many believe that the basic premise of psychology is cause/effect. For every effect, there must be a precipitating cause. All behavior is intrinsically motivated. Why is he drinking alcohol excessively? Why is he taking drugs? Why did his wife choose to become unfaithful? Why do I argue so easily? Our society has a tendency to look at the effect rather than the cause. A number of years ago, there was a media campaign on television to encourage young people to "just say no" to drugs. Obviously, most of us support efforts to stop this repugnant, self-destructive practice but the problem is much more complex than saying no. We have suggested that all "interpretive energy" must have a source. As stated previously, this is true of any effect, whether it be depression, lust, guilt, and/or yes, an argumentative spirit. Once we determine the source, we must begin the process of defining ("breaking it down") and understanding it.

20

(2) **It takes little for individuals to become inoperable.** I would like to draw upon the analogy of an automobile. My car can be a jalopy or a new Cadillac. If the battery is dead, it will not function.

If I smoke three packs of cigarettes a day, or have a drink or two between work and home, or have a little affair with the secretary, or argue with my wife occasionally and hit her; regardless of the dysfunction, the problem becomes the "foci" point. It can become both obsessive and compulsive. There is both a driving and controlling factor. I am not picking on cigarette smokers, but I recall while in graduate school being nudged by a fellow student who "couldn't wait until the class was over so they could have a smoke." I once did a seminar at a little country church. After the Sunday School hour, the majority of the men left the building. I commented to the pastor, "I hope it's not me." He laughed and said "come to the door," I looked out and half the men of the church were having a smoke between Sunday School and Church.

(3) **God created humans with parts.** The scriptures refer to them as members. As this particular word is used within the Bible, it primarily means "parts of the body". Some have established the argument that the word is physiological not psychological. Passages such 1 Corinthians 12: 12 states, " . . .the body is one and hath many members . . ." The verse is forming an analogy of gifts within the Church to different parts of the human body. The passage continues that "the eye cannot to say to the hand that I have no need to thee . . ." (1 Corinthians 12: 16). However, there are other verses where the

21

same Greek word is used that have strong psychological ramifications. Romans 6:19 challenges us not to yield our "members" to "become servants to uncleanness and to iniquity . . ." but to "yield our members to become servants to righteousness and holiness . . ." Are you ready to get excited? Notice first, that obviously the context of "members" here is more than physiology, but secondly, notice that the results desired, yea demanded by the Lord, are righteousness and holiness. Holiness – the desire to emulate God's character and righteousness –the desire to emulate God's standard. God desires to get some semblance of holiness and righteousness from us. James 4:1 reminds us that wars and fighting come from "lusting and warring within our members . . ." The last time I checked, my arms and legs were not bickering, but there have been times in my life that I have argued and have gotten mad; the energy had to come from somewhere.

(4)   **Our members interact and are interdependent.** None of these parts stand alone. I have the privilege of teaching a course entitled "Marriage and Family" at the college. We discussed, among items, gender differences and interpersonal relationships. For some reasons, these eighteen to twenty-two year-olds are intrigued with the opposite sex. Strange, isn't it? But I love to ask, "What attracts you to the opposite sex? Is it instinct (mating)? Is it sensual (sight, smell, etc . . .)? Is it emotional (love)? Or is it drive-oriented (sex)? They are such a great group.

And to continue the illustration, each of these parts is involved in dating. Each can stand alone, but usually all "intuitively interact" without consciousness on your part.

Let's relate this to an argumentative spirit. Proverbs 16: 32 states, "he that is slow to anger is better than the mighty; and he that rules his spirit than he that takes a city." Note the correlation between emotions ("slow to anger"), will ("rules"), and the spirit ("his spirit"). Here are three "parts" of personality interacting to control anger and the argumentative spirit. We are on the verge of our first insight in "healing" anger. What Biblical principles are pertinent to rebuilding the emotions, the will, and the spirit? The challenge for the Biblical counselor is to "restructure" the individual in these areas.

(5)   **There is perfection (completeness) within each of the parts.** Hebrew 12: 23 relates that the "spirit of the just man" may be "made perfect." How does a functional (or perfect) spirit differ from a dysfunctional one? If there is a pathological problem within an individual, how does that affect the human spirit? Can problems of the human spirit be diagnosed as part of the problem? How does all of these affect anger? We will eventually address these questions.

Let's consider one more illustration. Hebrews 9:9, in discussing sacrifices and gifts, states, "they could not make him that did the service perfect, as pertaining to conscience." Is it possible to have a perfect conscience? Now be careful...that thought could really be stimulating? How would this relate to guilt and peace?

It would seem that the potential for "completeness' is within all of us.

(6) **There is perfection within the whole.** Can you imagine victory over your argumentative spirit? Can we imagine a perfect spirit, a perfect conscience . . .? Hebrews 13 :21 relates that God desires to "make you perfect in every good work to do His will, working in you that which is well pleasing in His sight, through Jesus Christ; to whom be glory for ever and ever." God wants to "make us perfect in every good work to do His will...!" There is a constant refining process within us. Our lack of understanding and discernment fuel the devil's workings, and through his "principalities and powers", He continues to wound saints and attempts to keep the Church inordinate and ineffective. We want to change the emphasis from the wound to the healing. As you are reading through this material, God sees you healed. Envision a different person, diffused from anger and an argumentative spirit.

God works through a "purging" process. John 15:2 expounds that principle, "Every branch in me that beareth not fruit he taketh away; and every branch that beareth fruit, he purgeth it, that it may bring forth more fruit." I live in the country ... kind of... We have some trees and scrubs. Recently, I had to "purge" some limbs attacked by insects. They had eaten the leaves. I am amazed how something blossoms after it has been purged. Be ready not only for some changes but perhaps also be ready for some pain.

(7) **There has to be a structure.** Whether as individuals or as counselors, it is imperative that we have understanding of the structure of man. How did God create us? Do we have parts? How are these parts inter-related? Is there an inter-dependence? When the parts become "maladaptive", what are the consequences?

Your suggested structure is shown on the following page

Stop Arguing With Me

HOLY SPIRIT

Spirit - furnace

MONITOR

Conscience - imprintation

Emotion   Will

Faith

Memory   Energy   Intellect

Soul - interprets

DRIVES

Body – frame

Senses   Appearance   Instincts   Temperament

FLESH

(8) **The Parts can be defined**. Let's review. We all have tensions that manifest energy. This energy must have a source. Thus, there must be a structure within us. We have parts and the potential for perfection, or completeness, within these parts. If there is the potential for perfection within the parts, then there must be the potential for completeness within the whole. Thus, these parts can be defined:

Spirit ------------ is the furnace, the essence of life within man

Soul ------------- is the interpretative part of our personality

Conscience ---- is God's imprintation, potential for goodness

Emotions ------ are our feelings

Memory -------- is the storehouse of all our experiences

Faith Energy --- is the vacuum, or void, of personality

Intellect -------- is the potential for "reflective" thought

Will ------------- is the determiner

Body ------------ is the frame

Temperament ---------- is the genetic, the predisposition

Instincts -------- are our distinctives

Senses ----------- are the doors and windows

Appearance ------------- is our image

Drives ------------ are our urges

We will eventually discuss how these interact in expressing argumentation.

(9)   **And finally, parts within this structure can be "adaptive" or "maladaptive."** I am indebted to William Kirwan from his book, *Biblical Concepts of Christian Counseling*. He related:

"When Adam fell, genuine needs were born. The need to belong, the need for self-esteem, and the need for control are now the most prominent driving forces of personality. Do we meet our needs in the positive ways that God has designed, thus producing happiness and fulfillment, or do we try to meet our needs in our own way, which ultimately leads to self-destruction? We would like to think that we meet our needs God's ways. Mavis notes two inner forces which incline us to wrongdoing as we attempt to meet our needs: first, there are the natural and inborn tendencies, which the theologians have termed original or innate sin. Secondly, there are REPRESSED COMPLEXES AND MALADAPTIVE IMPULSES, which have been acquired in life experiences. Maladaptive impulses are qualitatively different from natural (original) sin. We all have legitimate needs and legitimate impulses to meet these needs. We also have a tendency toward sinful ways. Maladaptive impulses seek the normal ends of life (needs) ... wrongly."

He continues by identifying these "infirmities" within us. "The sincere person on the Christian quest becomes confused and disillusioned when he/she fails to recognize that the Holy Spirit does not cleanse away, like a great divine

28

psychiatrist, all the emotional complexes, defense mechanism, anxieties, and other ineffective psychological process when He fills the human heart with His sanctifying presence. Paul recognized that many of the psychic processes remain in the heart after the filling of the Spirit. After describing personal freedom in the law of sin and death in Romans 8, Paul says, 'Likewise the Spirit also helpeth our infirmities (Romans 8:26).' The Holy Spirit employs a different kind of divine therapy in resolving the acquired tendencies to wrongdoing. He does not remove all of them by an act of cleansing, but rather He helps believers to gain insight into their maladjustments and to resolve them by His strengthening process."

I've got news for you. All of us to some extent are "maladaptive." The emphasis of this material is on anger and an argumentative spirit, but certainly there can be many ways that these "maladaptive instincts" might express themselves. My heritage was one of anger. I had a strong-willed father, and the end result was that "maladaptive instincts" of strong will and anger were created within me. I developed an argumentative spirit. Note that this is an "instinct." I began a process of building defenses and walls to survive. We normally don't consciously articulate instincts. If we are happily married, instinctively how much do we focus on concepts such as companionship, encouragement, and security? But within our marital relationships, these concepts are there. And if there is a vacuum within us and needs are unmet, we might become angry and enraged and argumentative.

Self-realization is the first step of change. Let's close the chapter by taking the following test. Are we adaptive or maladaptive?

Adaptive/Maladaptive Behavior

Chart to evaluate adaptive/maladaptive behavior. Each statement is worth ten points. Add up the number of points. Grade yourself from 1 – 10, with 10 being the highest. Grading Scale 90 – 100 = A; 80 – 89 = B; 70 – 79 = C, 60 – 69 = D; Below 60 = F.

(1) Am I more optimistic than pessimistic in my outlook on life? Do others perceive me to be cheerful and encouraging? (MY SPIRIT)_____

(2) Am I a "sweet" person to be with? Is there a minimal amount of bitterness and cynicism from life? (My Soul)_____

(3) Do I have an inner peace in my life and generally feel comfortable with my relationship with God and others? Do I have a minimal amount of guilt? (MY CONSCIENCE)_____

(4) Do others perceive me a s a loving and happy person? Do I have a minimal amount of anger and fear in my life? (MY EMOTIONS) _____

(5) Do I live in the present? Am I excited about what is presently happening in my life, or is there a tendency to be

pre-occupied with experiences from the past? (MY MEMORY) _____

(6) Do I have an active and personal faith that is lived and practices, or I am pre-occupied with "addictive" behavioral tendencies such as cigarettes, alcohol, gambling, etc? (MY FAITH ENERGY) _____

(7) Do I respond well to correction? Would others not consider me a strong willed person? (MY WILL)_____

(8) Do I have a self acceptance of my body? Do I believe that God did not make mistakes when He made me? (MY APPEARANCE) _____

(9) Do I keep my body under subjection? Do I have will power when it comes to eating or sexual struggles? (MY BODY)

_____

(10) Do I understand my own temperament and "hows and whys" as to my general responses to pressures, people, and struggles? (MY TEMPERAMENT) _____

My score is _____; My grade is_____

3

Spirit-Soul Complexity

Where does anger and argumentation begin? How is it expressed? It is complex to understand the "marriage" of our spirit/soul/body. And certainly in the dichotomy/trichotomy debate, there are Scriptures where the terms spirit and soul are interchangeable. This chapter is our last preliminary chapter before we specifically expound how to heal the argumentative spirit. A better understanding of our "spirit" and "soul" are imperative in this quest.

I first met her in a "protective" home." Her husband was out on bond. She had "caught" him in an affair. He was apologetic, begged for forgiveness, and promised her that he would never do it again. She took him back and seemingly they were reconciled. Some three weeks later, he related that he wanted to take her to a nice restaurant in Ann Arbor, Michigan. She was to wear her finest clothes. They had a "seemingly"

33

enjoyable meal, and they were on their way home. Suddenly, he pulled the car unto a back road. To quote her exactly, as she related it to me, "Dr. Cuthbertson, I thought that I was going to be romanced." But, in fact, her husband looked at her with "rage" pouring from his eyes and related that he was going to kill her. He began to pound her across the face with his fists. She was able to get the car door open. He ran around the car, tackled her, and as she was in absolute hysteria, he held her down with his knees on her arms and proceeded to hit her "back and forth" across the face. In his perverted mind, his intent was to knock her out, place her behind the steering wheel, and push the car over a hill that dropped into the Huron River. Another car had been "stashed" away for him to make his escape. His plans, however, went awry. When he pushed the car toward the crest of the hill, a small bush kept the car from going over the hill. At about this same time, another car drove up upon the scene, and he had to leave.

In the next scene, she is in a coma at the University of Michigan hospital. The husband was by her side, well aware that if she comes "out of" this coma, he is "fried." A suspicious sister stayed with her continually. In one of the few moments, when he was out of the room, she did come out of the coma in absolute hysteria. He was arrested. He was out on bond (if you can believe that). She was placed in a "safe house." It was through the sister that I was drawn into this.

I related to my wife that listening to her story was devastating. As she shared the details with me, she cried incessantly. She was frightened: she was depressed. She was a broken lady. I will never forget her final comment as she concluded the story. In sobbing outcries, she blurted, "You see, it is not so much what he did to my body, it is what he did to my spirit."

She was correct. Proverbs 15:4 states that, "A wholesome tongue is a tree of life, but perverseness therein crushes the spirit." Her spirit had been crushed. As clinicians, we will meet patients who have had experiences so traumatic that their spirit is wounded, or crushed, or afflicted.

Now, back to our tragic story, when it was over (he did eventually go to prison), what do you think she felt? Do you suppose that there was any anger or rage within her? Now reflect for a moment. Perhaps your life has not been quite so dramatic, but "your narrative life" has had many diverse experiences. What have been the effects?

In this chapter, I will develop Biblical principles of the human spirit and soul. First, let's consider some principles of the human spirit.

(1) **The human spirit is the essence of life within us.** The human sprit is the furnace. In Genesis 2:7, the spirit is defined as the "breath of life", breathed into man by God. When we die, our spirit is released. Note that when Jesus gave up His spirit to the Father (Luke 21:46), he died. James 2:26 relates that the "body without the spirit is dead ..." . We are alive because we have this "furnace", this energy source, within us. We are not empowered by the local power company. There are no cords

running from us into the wall. We are an entities within ourselves. Are you getting excited yet? Proverbs 20:27 (NASB) relates that "the spirit of man is the lamp of the Lord, searching all the innermost parts of his being." A study of words like "candle, lamp, and light" within Scripture many times relates to this dimension of personality. Vine's *Expository Dictionary of Biblical Words* defines spirit as "the life principle, bestowed upon man by God." Frank Minirith in his book *Christian Psychiatry* expounds the spirit as "being the supernatural part of man given by God at birth". The definition I like best, however, comes from Frank Deiltsch in his book *A System of Biblical Psychology*. He states, "The spirit which was breathed into man was indeed, the condition of life to his body." The words "condition of life" intrigued me. You see the body of a person, but you perceive a "persona", a personality. In reality, your conclusion of the person comes basically from his or her spirit.

Personality theorist Gordon Allport calls this energy source the "propriate." To him, this was the "motivational factor for the mature adult." It was his word for ego or self; it comprised the "core" of personality. To Gordon Allport, there must be an essence of life from which energy originates. To the founder of psychoanalysis, Sigmund Freud, this "propriate" was called "instinct." He assumed that functions of the body are carried out through "energy," psychic energy. He stated, "The human instinct was the basic unit of personality. It is the motivation, propelling force of personality that not only drives behavior but also determines its direction." These personality theorists I contend are defining the Biblical concept of spirit - the essence of life within us.

(2) **The human spirit can be characterized.** I delight in teaching this at college. I have the students take out a small piece of paper that is turned immediately back to me nameless. I challenge them "to characterize themselves in one word." I collect the papers and before the class in animated fashion conjure students who have put a "negative" word on the paper. I extol those who have put down positive words such as "loving, happy, cheerful, optimistic, etc ... " Now come on ... how do some people get so negative, and others are so positive? What word would you use to characterize your spirit?

I challenge you to write it down _____

We characterize people through their spirits. When I was in seminary, I pastored a small, local church. After my first sermon, I was greeting people at the door. To a particular lady (now deceased), I made the mistake of inquiring, "How are you today?" I will not soon forget her "organ recital." I learned never to ask again. Now don't misunderstand; using this illustration does not mean that we should not be understanding and loving to hurting people. However, we must not only be able to step back and analyze the human spirit, but we must understand the "etiology" of such.

The Bible speaks of "haughty" spirits (Proverbs 16: 18) and of "humble and contrite spirits (Isaiah 66:2). Proverbs 17: 27 states, "He that hath knowledge spares his words and a man of understanding is of an excellent spirit." Are you getting excited yet? The Hebrew word is "*yagar*," which among possible renderings is the word "cool." It doesn't quite follow teenage vernacular, but it does have an "awesome" meaning. It implies that when others are upset and when circumstances are confusing, that there is at least one person who is "under control." His furnace is not heated up. He is "cool." Let's take it a step further. In 1 Peter 3:4, the Christian wife is exhorted to have a "gentle and quiet spirit." The Greek word for "quiet" can be translated "mild, tranquil, or peaceable." Here is a lady who can sustain a cool, quiet spirit in the face of adversity. The challenge for this material on argumentation is to obtain this.

(3) **We worship and learn in the spirit.** John 4:24 states that "God is a Spirit, and they that worship Him must worship in spirit and in truth." Psychologically, the passage relates that change is dependent upon attitude. I can go to church and not really be there in "spirit." I can go to school and not be a student. If I do not have an attitude of learning, change, and resolve, changes will not ensue.

I recall dramatically an incident that occurred toward the conclusion of my master's degree program. A professor, being a bit of a "free spirit," decided to pull two students to the front of the class and let the rest of the class "analyze" them. This was a secular university. I knew when he introduced this project that I would be chosen (and I was). The students were encouraged to make various observations of Mr. Davis and myself. When the class had finished, the professor decided to make his comments. He began (with a smile), "Duane, your biggest problem is that you have come to this class not as a student but as a teacher; I will tell you how you give yourself away. When you ask questions of me, you preface them with the words, 'don't you think' or 'don't you agree.' You are not asking me questions; you are trying to manipulate me into your conclusion." I will never, never forget those comments. At the ripe old age of 23, I was not a student. Are you still a student? Can anyone correct you? We all can be shocked by our own "self deception."

(4) **The human spirit is the first point of change.** People must have a desire to change. Bless you. You have purchased this book. Do you really want to deal with the angry and argumentative spirit? Do you really want to become a different person? A teacher shook a little boy adamantly and pushed him down into the chair. The boy's face coiled with rebellion and glaring, he responded, "in my body I am sitting down, but in my spirit, I am still standing up."

Conversely, we will "prove" that the soul is the "interpretive" part of our personality. In the Old Testament, the Hebrew word "nephesh" was used some 171 times basically, but not inclusively, to relate to the life principle in both animals and human (Genesis 1 :20,24,etc). But in both the Old and New Testament, the soul in different places was equated to human personality. In Proverbs 13:4, note that the soul desired, "... the soul of a lazy man desires and has nothing ... " Matthew 16:25-26 states, "For whosoever will save his life shall lose it, and whosoever will lose his life for my sake shall find it. For what is a man profited, if he shall gain the whole world and lose his own soul? or what shall a man give in exchange for his soul?" Let's consider these principles concerning the soul:

(1) **The spirit and the soul are distinct.** There are a number of passages that explore this uniqueness. In the Old Testament, Isaiah 26:9 states, "... with my soul have I desired thee in the night; yea with my spirit within me will I seek thee early." In the New Testament, Luke 1:46-47, Mary during her pregnancy with Jesus proclaimed, "my soul does magnify the Lord, and my spirit hath rejoiced in God my Savior". There are three distinct words in the Greek for spirit (pneuma), soul (psychos), and body (sarkos). There is not only "interaction" within the spirit/soul, but there is "interaction" within the parts of the soul. An example of this is Deuteronomy 4:9 "take heed, keep thy soul diligently, lest thou forget things thine eyes have seen ... lest they depart from thy heart." This is such an "awesome" passage relating how our memory and emotions are within the soul. We will study this more in depth later.

(2) **The soul, as the spirit, can be characterized.** We know that the soul can be depressed. Did not Jonah cry unto the Lord to "please take my life (Jonah 4:3)." It can express anguish. David in Psalm 116:4 stated, "Oh Lord, I implore you, deliver my soul." The soul can be bitter. Job wailed in Job 3:20, "Wherefore is light given to him that is in misery, and life unto the bitter in soul." On the positive side, David loved Jonathan "as his own soul (I Samuel 18:1, 3), and the satisfaction that the Lord can "redeem my life from distress (I Kings 1:29)."

Perhaps Jacob's condemnation on his sons Simeon and Levi is the best example of anger (Genesis 49:5-7). These two sons were described as being cruel (v.5). They were so angry and so cruel that they killed a man and lamed an ox. He stated in verse seven, "cursed be their anger, for it was fierce, and their wrath, for it was cruel (v.7)."

Do others see anger, rage, and argumentation within us? Let's continue...

(3) **The soul is the interpretive part of our personality.** It has long been my contention that it is not what happens to us, it is how we interpret it. No person, no situation, no circumstance is anymore of a threat to us than what we make it. As we move toward the "healing" process of our argumentative spirit, our soul obviously must help in initiating the change."

As stated, it was my privilege to pastor a Swedish Covenant Church while attending seminary. There the Lord allowed many dear, dear saints to minister to me. Mrs. Almstrom was one of them. She had arthritis so badly she could hardly walk but she was there for every church function. On Sunday mornings, the "elder" folk had Sunday school on the first level of the church. Some steep stairs had to be "negotiated" for the sanctuary and the worship service. For Mrs. Almstrom, this was painful. The grimace of pain was observed in each step. One Sunday, I met Mrs. Almstrom at the top of the steps (she refused to let me help her), and stated, "that must be awfully painful." Her response was, "Oh no, oh no, pastor you must realize that it is not my pain, it is God's pain,

41

He is only giving to me the privilege of feeling it." It is never what happens; it is always how we interpret it.

Scripturally, a good example of this would be the principle in Proverbs 22:5, "Thorns and snares are in the way of the perverse; he who guards his soul will be far from them." Notice how the "soul" is aware of the temptation and the distortion, but he "protects" his soul from them. And then, of course, the next verse challenges us to "train up a child in the way he should go, and when he is old, he will not depart from it." The spirit, soul, and body must be trained. When we are lax in such training, it can lead to people being weak and wounded, which can make them susceptible to argumentation. The soul is the "seat of our appetites." Psalms 107:9 relates that "God satisfies the longing soul and fills the hungry soul... " Do you have any longings that you want filled? The soul is also the "seat of our minds." Deuteronomy 26:16 states, "The Lord your God commands you to observe these statutes and judgments; therefore, be careful to observe them with all your heart and with all your soul."

(4) **God desires "perfection" in our spirit and soul.** Passages such as Hebrews 12:23, Job 9:21, and James 1:4 make clear that God wants us to become "perfect and entire, wanting nothing." As we are struggling with flesh on any level, we have choices as to how we interpret the struggles in our life and how we feed our spirits. Hold on.... We will now attempt to prove our premise that the argumentative spirit can be healed.

4

Argumentative People are Sick –
Defended

nger and argumentation are correlated. Why do we have to retort? Why do we have to prove that we are right? Proverbs 16:32 states, "He that is slow to anger is better than the mighty, and he that rules his spirit can take a city." At the close of this material, you will be able to rule your spirit. Now conversely, in my life's journey, if I had a quarter for every argument I have had in my life... Indeed I have heard my wife say many times, "You have to have the last word, don't you? She is right. But in all candor, there is "something" in my mind that impedes me considering the "rightness" of your thoughts. As you are talking, I am thinking rebuttal. There was something in my mind (this is changing), that impedes me considering the "righteousness" of your thoughts. I am only considering retort. I am thinking, "Go ahead and finish and I will tell you where you are wrong,"

It started with my sin nature. We must recognize that because of sin, "we have a force within us that is capable of controlling us, reigning over us, and using us as instruments of unrighteousness." As stated in chapter one, Psalms 51:1-2 states, "Have mercy on us, o God, according to thy loving-kindness, according unto the multitude of thy tender mercies, blot out my transgressions, wash me thoroughly from mine iniquity and cleanse me from my sin." We know from this passage that our sin nature has at least three parts. The word "sin" means that we have "missed the mark." The word "iniquity" means that we are "bent away from God." Our argumentative spirit comes from the word translated "transgression." The Hebrew word is "pesha". We are in a "state of rebellion." It is much easier to be negative than positive, argumentative than quiet. It is within our very nature.

It was reinforced through my genetic predisposition. Some of us are more "predisposed" to arguing and anger. As previously stated, we know from Psalm 139 that God has placed the "bent" within each child. I believe that of the four basic temperaments irritable, defiant, sensitive, and compliant, the irritable and defiant people are more prone to anger. However, I also believe (my wife has taught me), that a sensitive or compliant person, whose "spirits" have been crushed (Proverbs 15:4), can become "fighters." Intuitively they think, "I have taken enough." They individualize. They change. The irony is that many times now, the instigator does not understand. Tragically, in some cases now the argumentation becomes more intense.

It is reinforced by my gender. Studies relate that men are worse. Dr. Mark Cogsgrove in an article, "***The Anger Difference***" comments:

"Brain differences between the sexes can lead men and women to view anger-producing situation with different mindsets. These same brain differences can also predispose men and women to choose certain responses to anger rather than others. In general, women are more likely to display a wider range of emotion in anger than are men. This does not just mean that women cry more when angry, which they do. Women are also more likely than men to verbalize their angers and reasons for their angers. Men, on the other hand are more likely than women to be aggressive in anger situations."

Dr. Cogsgrove gives three defenses: (1) brain differences, (2) hormonal differences, and (3) social differences. He continues...

"Recent studies reveal that female brains are "net like" in that they show more elaborate connections in all cortical areas. The female also has a proportionately larger corpus callosum than the male, which also increases emotional and verbal interconnections in all areas of the female brain. Male brains by contrast ... have less circuitry connecting the centers. One result of such brain differences is that the female brain seems more personal and detail oriented. The male brain, by contrast, offers a less personal, more abstract view of the world. It is easier for the male to see people as objects ... that may lead him into acts of greater violence and aggression. Women by contrast are more likely to use their verbal superiority than muscles to attack, and they will continue arguments internally long after confrontations."

"Higher male hormonal levels are also implicated in male aggressiveness and more overt expressions of anger .... the male hormone testerone is implicated in this. Men generally have 10 times the level of testosterone in their bodies than women have ... Both sexes get angry, but the flood of testosterone in male pushes harder against men toward certainly more anger expressions ... Although a flood of testosterone does not guarantee aggression and anger, it does provide the rush of energy that males can use for aggressive purposes."

"Society also conditions or at least reinforces already existing biological differences between men and women. Our culture does in some ways free the male to engage in more overtly aggressive anger. Women, who feel just as angry, learn to show less direct expressions of anger. Society often expects little girls to be nice and sweet and never angry. Society may not encourage aggressive displays in young males, but aggression is more discouraged in young females. Society, therefore, reinforces some of the natural inclinations of men and women with regard to external aggression verses verbal and indirect expressions of anger."

Thus, it starts with a "triggering" within our spirits. No one starts out with a life ambition of becoming a drunk or a prostitute, or an argumentative person. Most struggles are progressive. The man who starts with social drinking does not perceive himself as a drunk. The person begins with a basic curiosity, but one day finds himself entrenched in pornography. In this evolutionary process, there is a "triggering" mechanism. Somewhere, the struggles become both obsessive and compulsive. Thus, I believe that mental illness goes through five stages: (1) We have a sin nature predisposed for our demise, (2) We become self-centered, (3) We become defensive, (4) We "trigger" mental illness, and (5) We reinforce our sickness. Now remember, "self realization" is the first step of change.

Let's consider the etiology of "argumentative" sick people. It has two steps:

People with an argumentative spirit have a "fractured spirit." Throughout this study, we will analyze the context of contention in the Scriptures. Romans 2:6-11 says, "God will render to every man according to his deeds. To them who by patient continuance in well doing seek for glory and honour and immorality, eternal life. But unto them that are contentious and do not obey the truth, but obey unrighteousness, indignation, and wrath. Tribulation and anguish upon every soul of man that doeth evil of the Jew first and also of the Gentile. But glory, honor, and peace, to every man that worketh good, to the Jew first, and also to the Gentile. For there is no respect of persons with God."

The Greek work for "contention" here is "erithera", which among possible translations means a "fractured spirit." Now if that seems a bit abstract, remember that in the study of

MPD (Multiple Personality Disorders), it is concluded that patients can not only have different personalities within them, but each of these personalities can have his/her own memory. Within our study of "Stress Anthropology", how is that possible, and how is this energy manifested?

It gets a bit more ironical in that there is a disease called "erethism" taken from this Greek word. It basically relates to an individual who has "morbid energies, hyperactive, and restless." It presently relates to the effect of "mercury toxicity" upon the individual. It is an amalgam-related illness (FAQ). Among the symptoms manifested is irritability, outbursts of temper, and stress intolerance. It also relates to the sexual effects of certain drugs upon some individuals. It relates to a hyper alertness and hyper sexuality.

Now, folks when you get as old as I am, you can take certain liberties. The psychological and physiological communities at this point have missed it; the theological community has it correct. The word is translated "contentious". There has been a "fracturing" within the spirit that has led to an illness. Can we comprehend that excessive arguing can be illness? There has been a "fracturing" within the spirit that has led to an illness. **People who argue excessively are indeed sick.** Let's consider, scripturally, some of the manifestations of this illness.

(1) **The spirit can be agitated.** Proverbs 15:13, "A merry heart maketh a cheerful countenance, but by sorrow of heart the spirit is broken (agitated)." The Hebrew word literally means to

"smite" or "afflict" - an instant sharp pain. Lewis Smedes in his book, *The Art of Forgiving* discusses two types of hurts. The first one he calls the hurt of "disloyalty." He defines this as "when someone who belongs to you treats you like a stranger." Have you ever felt slighted, or abandoned, or neglected? How did this affect your spirit? Did it "color" your attitudes of trust or confidence? The second hurt Dr. Smedes calls the hurt of "betrayal." During this stage, individuals choose to "cut you into pieces." Have you ever had anyone turn on you with such force that you were "cut to pieces?" How did it affect you?

(2) **The spirit can be wounded.** Proverbs 18:14 states, "The spirit of a man will sustain his infirmity, but a wounded spirit, who can bear it?" This is the same Hebrew word from above, but it now has a stronger intensity. Through counseling for over 30 years, I have heard many stories. I will not soon forget a young lady relating how her alcoholic father, threw a meal that her mother had prepared to the floor, and in the presence of the children, grabbed his wife by the back of the neck and made her eat the food from the floor. Can we conjecture the possible affects of this upon children? What did they feel? What did they think about marriage, relationships, and love? Would it wound the spirit?

(3) **The spirit can be crushed.** Proverbs 15:4, "A wholesome tongue is a tree of life but perverseness therein is a breach (crushes) the spirit." This is a much stronger word, meaning to break, crush, or even destroy. I had a cousin who was captured by the Chinese in the Korean War. He was in captivity for some two years, and during that time, his spirit was crushed. Before

going into the service, he was a happy, jovial individual. After the war, he became a quiet, solemn individual. I remember asking him, "What happened?" He related that if I had gone through what he had experienced, I would not be the same either. I don't doubt some of you have had experiences so traumatic that your spirit has been crushed.

(4) **The spirit can become haughty.** Proverbs 16:18 says, "Pride goeth before destruction and a haughty spirit before the fall." The Hebrew word for haughty means "lofty and prideful." The individual can't be told anything.

I recall a counseling situation so severe that the husband would not let the wife talk. He would literally not let her finish a sentence without interrupting and "correcting" her.

(5) **The spirit can become argumentative.** Proverbs 29:1, "He that being often reproved hardeneth his neck, shall suddenly be destroyed and that without remedy." The word "hardeneth" means stiff-necked and unmovable. The individual has regressed intuitively to the point that no matter the issue, he/she is ready to counter and be argumentative.

A lady came to the counseling session intent on changing her husband. She assaulted him openly during the first session. He sat quietly, realizing any attempted retort would be futile. I opened the second session by relating that I would not be meeting with them further. "But why?" she stated. "Well," I retorted, "If we continue counseling, Mrs._____, I will eventually have to relate that you are part of the problem, and you will not respond well; so it is best for us to discontinue now." She immediately got up, agreed with me, took her husband's hand and left. People with argumentative spirits generally are not open to correction. This topic will eventually be discussed. Who corrects you?

(6) **The spirit can become closed.** There is not a definite passage here, but I do think of the contention between Paul and Barnabas over Mark in Acts 15:24-41. Verse 39 relates that the contention was so sharp between them, that they departed asunder one from the other. Gary Smalley, in his book *The Key to Your Child's Heart*, has a good chapter on parents and children closing off their spirits from one another. On any level this could be a natural progression of the other "syndromes" discussed. If the irritation is so intense that the spirit is agitated, wounded, and crushed, the tendency might be to close off one's spirit. It can become a defensive posture to fight back.

So let's review.... If we have been wounded or crushed in our spirits, it is possible we have developed an argumentative spirit. We are calling the disease "erethism" taken from the Greek word translated "contentious." The very essence of life within us, our spirit, has become "fractured" and splintered. A "perceived attack" will "trigger" the disorder and we become angry, enraged, resentful, or indignant.

And we will eventually defend that this can be manifested in various degrees.

The second phase of the illness is the effect upon the soul. Remember the soul is our "interpretive" part. Right now ... as you are reading ... you are interpreting. Proverbs 13: 18 is such an "awesome" passage, "A desire accomplished is sweet to the soul..." Think with me of a "desire" that you accomplished. Remember your first house ... your college degree ... that special car. How did you feel? Notice that your soul was "sweet." The word literally means "pleasurable". You know when you are happy compared to when you are sad. Conversely, Proverbs 27:7 states, "A satisfied soul loathes the honeycomb, but to a hungry soul every bitter thing is sweet." The hungry soul tries to "cover" the bitterness. Perhaps if I get drunk enough ... high enough... but the bitterness is still there.

Your wounded spirit has affirmed a persona (a personality). Would others consider you positive, optimistic, loving, and happy? Or would others consider you negative, pessimistic, self centered, and sad? Your spirit "feeds" you soul.

Again, let's review the study of the word "contentious." The Hebrew word is "midyar" which among its various meanings is translated "ill tempered". Note the use of the word 'ill'. Our premise is that "people who argue are sick." Here are a couple of examples. Proverbs 21: 19, "It is better to dwell in the wilderness, than with a contentious and angry woman." You know these people when you meet them. They are "ill" tempered. When I was a child, I lived near a "contentious" woman. She stood guard by her home, and if any person's foot touched her lawn, she was out "growling." Tragically, kids being who they are, and the sinful nature being what it is, her property took a beating. Men also can be "ill" tempered. Proverbs 26:21 states, "As coals are to burning coals, and wood to fire, so is a contentious man to kindle strife." Let's remember that it is the fathers who are exhorted in Ephesians 6:4 not to "provoke our children to wrath ...". I remember a man during a counseling session relating that he would "pull" the spark plug wires in the car to keep his wife from going to church.

Let's consider four "personality types" that can be formed from a person sick with the disease "erethism". Check if any of these would describes you.

The Callused Person - (the indifferent person). This person is rash and wrathful. Proverbs 15:1, "A soft answer turneth away wrath, but grievous words" stir up anger." The Hebrew word here is "etseb". It means to be hurtful and to "inflict pain." They want to see the other person hurting. Another place where the word is used is Proverbs 15:18, "A wrathful man stirs up strife, but he that is slow to anger appeaseth strife." How much are you oblivious to the hurts of others? The number one criterion for mental health is to be able to see it from the other's perspective. For the callused, person this is very difficult.

The Crushed Person - (the sarcastic person) --- Proverbs 15:4, "A wholesome tongue is a tree of life, but perversion is a breach (crushing) of the spirit." The word perversion means "out of focus". A person with a crushed spirit is either quiet or responds back with sarcasm. As previously stated, this might be especially true of a sensitive person. If we return to our discussion of temperaments, I would classify myself as irritable (type A) and my wife as sensitive. You can appreciate that with the strength of my personality in the early days of our marriage, I crushed the spirit of my wife. She is wonderful, loving, caring, and compassionate, but ... after a few years of this, she began to resist. I had crushed her spirit and brought out her will.

The Contentious Person - (the nagging person) --- Proverbs 17: 14 says, "The beginning of strife is as when one letteth out water; therefore, leave off contention, before it be meddled with ... " This is a different word (riyh). This is a quarreling and disputing person. This is such a good analogy. Imagine watering your lawn, and then trying to get the water back through the hose. You can't be a quarreling person without having possible consequences. You will see it in your spouse and in your children.

The Chafed Person - (the avoidance person) --- Proverbs 18:19, "The brother offended (stepped on) is harder to be won than a strong city, and their contentions are like the bars of a castle." I think of a patient who was punished as a child by being locked in his room for weeks. Food was literally shoved through the door. This same person as an adult came home from work one day and found a note from his wife relating that she had left. He was so angry with his past experiences, that now he would hardly talk. My heart "hurt" for him.

Thus, your crushed spirit (erethism) has affected your soul, and you have become ill tempered. Your soul has taken on a negative persona. Others will observe this even if you do not. But a sovereign God had you begin reading this book because He wants to heal you. The steps of my own healing have been incredible. We will consider the consequences of this sickness for a couple chapters, investigate how this anger is expressed, and then we will begin, by God's grace, the healing process. So hold on.

Let's close the chapter with a test.

Let's test ourselves. Rate yourself 1-10 (ten the highest). Add your totals and grade accordingly: 90-100 - A, 80-89 - B, 70-79 - C, 60-69 - D, Below 60 - F.

1.   Would others consider you an argumentative person? ___

2.   Have you been hurt and wounded in the past?   ___

3.   Have you forgiven those who have given you pain?   ___

4.   Would you consider yourself a strong willed person?   ___

5.   Do you have a tendency to overreact to small problems?

        ___

6.   Did your parents argue excessively?   ___

7.   Do you generally "want to continue" an argument?   ___

8.   Have you had "crushing" experiences in your past?   ___

9.   Have you ever "struck" your spouse, children, or others in anger? ___

10.   Do you "internalize" your anger at times?   ___

Total   _____   Score   _____

5

Demons Occupy the Spirit

It is a sobering verse. Matthew 5:37 states, "But let your communication be yea, yea, nay, nay, for whatsoever is more than these cometh of evil (from the evil one)." This refers to Satan. Satan is not sovereign, but through his hordes of demons, he identifies through our words our weaknesses. And dearly beloveds, he attacks. He becomes conscious of our struggles, and he exploits them. Athletics are built around the same premise. As a former football and basketball player (oh so many years ago), I recall that we were constantly analyzing where our opponents were perceived to be vulnerable. Proverbs 7 gives to us an analogy of a prostitute, as Satan, enticing a young man. She sets the trap, she teases, she lies, and finally the young man is caught. The 22nd verse begins "He goeth after her straightway, as an ox goeth to the slaughter ... as a bird hasteth to a snare, and knoweth not that it is for his life ... for she hath cast down many wounded; yea, many strong men have been slain by her." I trust you caught that. He is wounded; he is vulnerable, and the devil is waiting to pounce. 1 Peter 5:8 exhorts us to "be sober, be vigilant, because your adversary the devil, as a roaring lion, walketh about, seeking whom he may devour." The word for 'devour' is swallow, and let's quickly note that Peter was writing to Christians. His comments are directed to either or both of the following: (1) some Christians who have already met the fate of being consumed, and/or (2) others who are ready to be consumed by their enemy, and Peter is warning of this occurring.

When Peter in Matt 16:22, "rebuked Jesus", Jesus retorted to Peter, "Get thee behind me Satan ... " Peter was striving to discourage Jesus from Calvary, and His ultimate crucifixion on the cross for our sins. Jesus immediately recognized that this was from Satan; however, the words were flowing from Peter's mouth.

Satan can and will use our words in attempting to "destroy" us. In II Corinthians chapter two, there had been some "dissention" over a brother in the church at Corinth. Paul exhorts the church to "confirm" their love for that brother (2:8) ... "lest Satan should get an advantage of us, for we are not ignorant of his devices." The Greek word for "advantage" not only connotes "to get gain" but also to "twine or braid" us. Note how that Satan is striving to utilize "situations" in our lives to bind and strangle us.

And now we are ready for the passage in Ephesians 4:26-27 that directly deals with Satan utilizing our argumentative spirit to get a "foothold" in our lives. The passage states, "Be ye angry, and sin not, let not the sun go down upon your wrath **neither give place to the devil**." The word for place means to "get a position" or "to get a home." Can it be any more obvious? Those of us who have argued into the night, have opened ourselves directly to demonic activity and inhabitation. And again, let's remember that this is written to the church. Praise God. We have no angry people in our churches. Amen.

The Bible gives to us a grotesque image of the devil and his demons. We know that Satan was at one time an angel in heaven (Ezekiel 28:11-19, Isaiah 14:12-14, Job 38:1-7). Apparently at one point in the past, he attempted to lead a rebellion in heaven against God (Revelation 12:7). He was defeated and the earth was given to him as his domain (Certainly, only God knows why.) He became the god of this world (Eph. 2:2, 11. Cor.4:4). In Satan's fall, he drew a vast number of angels with him (Revelation 12:4,9). Some of the fallen angels are loose and some are bound in a place called the Abyss (Luke 8:31). The loose ones we call "demons", or evil spirits. Of the bound ones, there are two kinds, permanently bound (2 Peter 2:4, Jude 6) and temporarily bound (Revelation 9:1-11). Satan and his demons now wage war against God's kingdom (Revelation 12:17). We know that demons can enter both people and animals (Luke 4 and Luke 8). In the story of "legion" in Luke, chapter 8, we know that the man was possessed with many evil spirits. We know that Satan is devoid of conscience and he is a liar (John 8:44). And unlike what is portrayed by Hollywood, the demons can appear in attractive forms. Demons are deceivers. They love to masquerade. Paul wrote to the Corinthians, and said that they had eagerly received evil spirits into their midst (2 Corinthians 11:4) in the form of false prophets and false apostles. Paul warned them that even "Satan himself masquerades as an angel of light. It is not surprising, then, if his servants masquerade themselves as "ministers of righteousness" (2 Corinthians 11: 14-15).

We know from the Scriptures that Satan tempts believers to disobedience (I Chronicles 21: 1-7), to lose faith in God (Luke 22:31-32, 1 Peter 5:8), lie (Acts 5:32), to be immoral (I Corinthians 7:5), to be preoccupied by the world (I John 2:15,2 Timothy 4:10), to be proud (I Timothy 3:6), and to be discouraged (I Peter 5:6,7,10)

Do we understand this demonization process? Merrill Unger in his book, **Demons in the World Today** said, "demonization is a condition in which one or more spirits or demons inhabit the body of a human being and can take complete control of their victim at will". By temporarily blotting out his consciousness, they can speak and act through him as their complete slave or tool. The inhabiting demon (or demons) comes and goes much like the proprietor of a house who may or may not be "at home". He may precipitate an attack. In these attacks, the victim passes from his normal state, in which he acts like other people, to an abnormal state ..."

Dearly beloved, this battle is real. For some 14 years, I directed a Youth for Christ chapter in Ami Arbor, Michigan. One day, I received a call from the director of Campus Crusade at the University of Michigan. "Duane", he related, "I need to ask you a question. What experiences have you had with demons?"

He continued, "I have a young lady that I strongly suspect is demonically possessed, and I need some help to verify this. Will you help?"

I responded favorably; so on a crisp November day, a young lady was brought to my office. She had graduated from King's College in New York, and she had come to University of Michigan to pursue a Master's degree in music. She had a strong, religious background. We eventually discovered that in the course of two weeks in the past that she had three compelling, traumatic experiences. She was "dropped" by her boyfriend, and her father was killed in a hunting accident, and a close brother was killed in a car accident. At that point, seemingly, the trauma was so intense that she became totally disoriented.

Our offices were in a small house; so the Campus Crusade's director chose to wait outside in the car.

We talked briefly, and then I suggested that I pray with her. She was sitting in a soft, cushioned chair, and I was in front of her in a metal chair. I did many things in dealing with her that day which would not be replicated in future settings. One mistake is that I wrapped my hands around the top of her wrists as we prayed. As I started into the prayer, I compelled any "evil spirits" that were within to identify themselves and leave her in

Jesus name. At this point in the prayer she shook and went into a seizure. I was not sure what I was doing, but what I now perceive to be the Holy Spirit within me started shouting at the evil spirits that indwelled her. In a few seconds the seizure subsided. Still holding her wrists, I related that we were going to do it again, and identically at the same point in the prayer, again she went into a seizure. At this point, again I began shouting, and suddenly a voice came from within her that said, "leave her alone, she is mine." There was a brief dialogue in which the demons argued that she did not want them to leave. The girl was shaking. Again, suddenly she went limp. Motivation overwhelmed reason. I began this a third time. As I started the prayer, suddenly this girl took on great power, and with my hands on the "top" of her wrists, I was lifted off the floor in my chair, and I was thrown against the wall. I was not hurt. The girl bolted from the house, ran past the waiting car outside, and continued about a half mile down the road, and there she collapsed. This incident did wonders for my theology. I must have read immediately a dozen books. I continued to be somewhat involved with the girl, and eventually six demons were released from within her.

Another incident impacted my theology. Ron was a good friend both in high school and college. It was my privilege to room with him two years in college. Ron claimed that he had an aunt in Pennsylvania who could tell the future. She was a Christian lady. Well, I was very young at the time and very skeptical. However, two incidents occurred during my high school years that "pricked" my curiosity. Ron's father was involved in an accident. The family was concerned about medical expenses, but the aunt "prophesied" that they would receive a large sum of money, which they did. His father also was diagnosed with cancer, and he was not expected to live. The aunt in Pennsylvania "prophesied" that the doctors were wrong, and that he would live a full life, which he did. While in college, Ron at the end of his sophomore year, was close to failing. He contacted this aunt, and she said that he would finish college, which he did. I related to Ron that if this lady ever came to their house for a visit, I would like to meet her. That happened, and still as a very young man, I queried her, "From where did you get this power?" Now please understand that I am convinced that she is a fine, Christian lady." Her answer, I will never forget. She related, "God has given to me the power to discern the spirits. There are many spirits in this world, both good and bad, and the most prominent good spirit is the Holy Spirit, that comes directly from God. But there are also many good and evil spirits in any setting."

This thought was reinforced in 1 John 4:1, where we are exhorted to "try the spirits" whether they are of God. Note that this is plural. The next verse continues, "Hereby know ye the Spirit (Holy Spirit) of God; every spirit that confesseth that Jesus Christ is come in the flesh is of God." Now help me folks. Is the implication not that there are other "good spirits" besides the Holy Spirit? Let's continue into the next verse, "And every spirit that confesseth not that Jesus Christ is come in the flesh is not of God, and this is that anti-christ, whereof ye have heard that it should come, and even now is already in the world."

Note that the notion of "detached" spirits is reinforced, some good and some evil, and that the "spirit" of the antichrist was active even in the first century.

Now we know from the Scriptures that God's Holy Spirit comes into our spirit. Jesus related to Nicodemus in John 3:6 as he was striving to understand the new-birth experience "that which is born of the flesh is flesh; and that which is born of the Spirit is spirit." Note the dynamics of the Holy Spirit and our spirit. Romans 8:16 relates that "the Spirit (Holy Spirit) itself beareth witness with our spirit (human spirit), that we are the children of God."

We are now ready to address the question, can evil spirits indwell believers? Partial defense for skeptics is the fourth verse of the 1 John 4 passage. It states, "ye are of God, little children, and have overcome them (evil spirits); because greater is he that is in you, than he that is in the world." As Christians, we do have the Holy Spirit within us, but this verse does not address whether evil spirits can also co-habitat the believer. We will eventually give to you a theory.

We do have examples from the Scripture of "Christians" who became demon possessed. In the Old Testament the strongest example is King Saul. We know that Saul was a believer (I Sam. 10:9). That passage relates that God changed Saul's heart. To argue that Saul was not a believer is to argue that God's Spirit would anoint an unbeliever (10:11,) and that God would anoint an unbeliever over His inheritance, the Jewish people. Furthermore, he was filled with the Spirit and

64

prophesied (10:9-13). These appear to be characteristics of a believer. Later, after sinning, he was tormented (demonized) by an evil spirit from the Lord (16:14). Note that God sent the evil spirit to Saul. Now folks, this implies many ramifications. God, obviously, can take control of evil spirits as He desires. We know that God can blind minds (2 Cor. 3:14 and Romans 11:7) and God can give people over to reprobate (distorted) minds (Romans 1:28). That should sober all of us a bit. Let's continue; the precise reason why Saul was invaded by a demon is nowhere directly indicated. It may have been that during his rebellion against God (I Samuel 15:23), the door was opened for this evil spirit. You will note that after David entered Saul's service, and when David would play his harp, the evil spirit would leave Saul (16:23).

The best examples in the New Testament were probably Ananias and Sapphira (Acts 5:1-11). It is assumed that Ananias and Sapphira were a part of the "believers" mentioned in 4:32-35. Of course, in the dialogue, we know that they tried to hold back their giving from God. The Scripture tells us that Ananias had let Satan "fill" his heart. This is the same Greek word used in Ephesians 5: 18 that challenges us as believers to be "filled" with the Holy Spirit. Seemingly, it has the same meaning here. Satan had control of Ananias, the believer, and caused him to lie to God.

There is an interesting passage in 1 Corinthians 5:1-5 of folks within the church of Corinth strongly engaged in fornication. Paul continues his comments concerning these people in verse five saying, "To deliver such a one unto Satan for the destruction of the flesh, **that the spirit may be saved in the day of the Lord Jesus.**" Ramifications of this will be considered later.

So in reality, we today have many Christians experiencing vexing problems and struggles which go beyond natural psychological and emotional infirmities. At the request of her sister many years ago, I visited a bed-ridden lady who had a "tic" disorder. She was a graduate of Moody Bible Institute, and with pillows tied to her bed, as we talked about the Lord, she had both hands and feet wailing back and forth.

I previously mentioned a book by Merrill Unger, *Demons and the World Today.* In the book, he defended that Christians could be "oppressed" but not possessed. There was such an avalanche of dissent that he changed his mind. Among the dissenters was Dr. Raymond Edmond, former president of Wheaton College. Dr. Edmond's firsthand experience with crude demonism, as a result of missionary labors in Ecuador, gave him an understanding of the subject sometimes not possessed by purely theoretical Bible interpreters. Dr. Unger rewrote the book under the title *What Demons Can Do to Saints.* In this book, he defended that Christians are vulnerable to demonic possession when the "believer's position in Christ is unguarded and the doors left wide open by flagrant disobedience and willful persistent sin." He continues, "Accordingly, the Scripture clearly reveals that the believer is absolutely protected from Satan and demons in his "position" before God in Christ by virtue of his salvation in Christ (Heb.2:3). However, as far as his "experience" is concerned, protection against demonic attack is only proportionate as the believer knows and believes in his position and makes realizable (sic) in his experience (Romans 6: 11). Similarly, in his position before God in Christ, the believer is a fully panoplied (defended) soldier against whom Satan and demons are powerless. But, in his experience, Satan and demons can and will penetrate the armor unless the Christian warrior uses every part of it in resisting the enemy's attack (Eph. 6:10-18). The situation may be compared to a man who owns a house. If he completely controls it and occupies it, no one, of course, can move in without his approval. But if he does not occupy all the rooms and is lax concerning who visits and how long they stay, he may soon find himself with an illegal dweller or two, who may prove very difficult to get rid of (sic)."

So Dr. Unger concluded that the Christian could be possessed. Demons could possess the body and the soul His comments are, "through crass indulgence of the old nature, demon powers can influence through his body and soul. In cases where the sin is of such a character that it goes beyond the old, nature, the demon may invade and cause upheaval and chaos in the believer through his body and soul. In this case, the child of God displays a kind of split personality. First, he speaks and acts through the Spirit, but then under the influence of the demon power when it is in control."

Let's close the chapter with some tints of controversy. From my experience in the hand-full of situations where I have observed demon-possessed Christians, the spirit is also involved. There was no question that the very "essence of life", the furnace if you please, was also involved in the demonic expression. How is this possible? Well, let's present this theory. In the discussion of dissociative identity disorders (multiple personality disorders), many psychologists believe that this disorder is so sophisticated that in time each, of the "alter personalities" will develop it's own memory bank. The memory, if you please, is split. This is both complicated and intriguing. I think this is precisely what happens to "demon-controlled" Christians. Last chapter, we defended that during the development of "erethism", the human spirit splits. And taking it a step further, when the spirit is split, I contend that evil spirits can indwell the believer in the "maladaptive" parts. Our passage in 1 Corinthians 5:5 says that the flesh was given over to Satan but the "spirit" was saved. The Holy Spirit will never totally be extracted, unless God, Himself, chooses to take the Holy Spirit from them. Part of the spirit is indwelt by evil spirits, and part of the spirit is indwelt by the Holy Spirit. Our works will be tested. We all eventually will face judgment. 1 Corinthians 3:15 states, "If any man's work shall be burned, he shall suffer loss, but he himself shall be saved; yet so as by fire." This implies, I know, that perhaps we will see Saul and Ananias & Sapphira in heaven.

Now, I have already defended that the human spirit can be crushed, wounded, and weakened. I have already defended that the soul can become bitter and harsh. The devil can, through his demons, attack and eventually conquer and indwell the Christian. The argumentative spirit within us becomes more compelling and obsessive. Let me quickly hasten to say that this is the exception and not the rule. I relate to the students at college that struggles are 90% psychological and 10% demonic.

Scripture does defend that "argumentation" and anger can affect both the spirit and the soul. Ecclesiastes 7:9 challenges us "do not hasten your spirit to be angry, for anger rests in the bosom of fools." Proverbs 22:24-25 states, " ... and with a furious man thou shalt not go, lest you learn his ways, and get a snare to your soul." I started this chapter with the words "it's sobering ..." Dearly beloved, it is sobering to realize that not only can we become sick and develop erethism, but that spirit of anger and argumentation can indwell us and we can become demonized.

6

The Curse of an Argumentative Spirit

In psychology, we call it "measured effects." Can we begin to calculate the effects of having an argumentative spirit? As a child, I met my grandfather Cuthbertson just once. I remember how angry he seemed. My response was to pull back from him. My father had an argumentative spirit. But dad, God bless him, as he got older, this subsided. He died at 93.

The question does arise whether are we coded by God transgenerationally? Psalms 139 relates that God "fashioned" us in our mother's womb and our "days are numbered." 11 Timothy 1:9 states that, "God saved us and called us with a holy calling, not according to our works but according to His purpose and grace before the foundation of the earth"? Let's believe that God has purpose and design to accomplish through these words. I believe that. But I also believe that I had a transgenerational curse of anger and argumentation placed within me.

Deuteronomy 30: 19-20 relates, "I call heaven and earth to record this day against you, that I have set before you life and death, blessings and cursing; therefore, choose life, that both you and your seed may live. . . " Note that the Lord gives both blessings and curses. Note that "blessings and curses" can be transgenerational "both thou and thy seed may live ... " In 1 Corinthians 11:29-30 is the warning of taking communion "unworthily". The Scriptures states, "for he that eateth and drinketh unworthily, eateth and drinketh damnation to himself, not discerning the Lord's body. For this cause many are weak and sickly among you, and many sleep." What a thought! Could there possibly be a correlation between a person's sickness and his taking the Lord's supper "unworthily"? And who is keeping these records? Well, God is, of course. Let's not soon forget that Galatians 5:7 warns us: "Be not deceived: God is not mocked: for whatsoever a man soweth, that shall he also reap. For he that soweth to his flesh shall of the flesh reap corruption, but he that soweth to the Spirit shall of the Spirit reap life everlasting." Grasping this concept is beyond understanding. God is keeping elaborate records.

Dr. Stuart Briscoe preached the best sermon that I ever heard preached. His thoughts were built around God's grace, God's mercy, and God's justice. Praise God, we will take all the grace He wants to give us. Amen. Praise God, we will take all the mercy He will pour upon us. Amen. Praise God for His justice. We want to get what's coming to us. Amen. Well ... wait a minute.

The Curse of an Argumentative Spirit

But beloveds ... all throughout the book of Proverbs, we have the contrast between the wise and foolish. Proverbs 11:29 states that, "he that troubles his own house shall inherit the wind, and the fool be servant to the wise at heart." There are going to be divine consequences of having an argumentative spirit. I know ... I have been there.

And the main vehicle for "curses and blessings" are words. How many times do we say "God bless you" without considering the ramifications? Proverbs 11:9 states, "The hypocrite with his mouth destroys his neighbor, and through knowledge the righteous will be delivered." Proverbs 15:4, as we have already quoted, says, "A wholesome tongue is a tree of life, but perverseness in it breaks the spirit." Proverbs 18:21 relates that "Death and life are in the power of the tongue, and those who love it will eat its fruit." Your words not only affect your outer person but also potentially the inner person of others - sobering indeed.

God does indeed "code" us transgenerationally. Exodus 20:5 says, " ... for the Lord thy God am a jealous God, visiting the iniquity of the fathers upon the children unto the third and fourth generation of them that hate me." I believe that I was the product of my grandfather's argumentative spirit. Deuteronomy 28: 1 says" ... if thou shall hearken diligently unto the voice of the Lord thy God all these blessings shall come on thee ... blessed be the fruit of thy body, fruit of the ground, and fruit of cattle ..." Our will is the determiner in part of whether we are blessed or cursed.

73

I would suggest the reading of Derek Prince's good book, *Blessing or Curses*, and I would further suggest a thorough study of Deuteronomy 27-28. Dr. Prince suggests five different types of curses:

Mental and Emotional Breakdowns--- It is perhaps difficult to imagine a God of grace and mercy that pre-determines "trans-generational" curses. But it must be understood that He is, as previously stated, also a God of justice. Watch the passages closely. Deuteronomy 28:28, "The Lord shall smite thee with madness (mental), and blindness (spiritually), and astonishment (panic) of heart." Verse 65, "but the Lord shall give thee there a trembling heart, and failing eyes, and sorrow (listless) of mind." We can only speculate how many mental and emotional struggles are correlated to curses.

Repeated and Chronic Diseases--- Deuteronomy 28:20, "The Lord shall send upon thee cursing, vexation and rebuke ... the Lord shall make the pestilence cleave unto thee ... the Lord shall smite thee with consumption, and with a fever, and inflammation, and with an extreme burning." Could this last one be hemorrhoids?

I do believe that the "coded tendencies" for certain physical disorders are within us.

Barrenness, a tendency to miscarry or related female problems--- Deuteronomy 28:18, "Cursed shall be the fruit of your body ... (or of the womb)" This could include the inability to conceive, a tendency to miscarry, failure to menstruate,

74

irregular menstruation, debilitating menstrual cramps, frigidity, cysts, tumors, or some other irregular functions within the reproductive process."

Breakdown of marriage and family alienation--- Note that many family struggles are transgenerational. Deuteronomy 28:41, "You shall begat sons and daughter, but they shall not be yours; for they shall go into captivity. There are many other strong prophesies built around the demise of the family. Malachi 4:5-6, "... before the coming of the great and dreadful day of the Lord, and he will turn the hearts of the fathers to the children and the hearts of the children to their fathers, lest I come and strike the earth with a curse." 11 Timothy 3:1-2, "This know also, that in the last days perilous times shall come. For men shall be lovers of their own selves, covetous, boasters, proud, blasphemers, disobedient to fathers ..." Let's not forget that the last of the "blessings promised" in Ephesians 6:1-3 is related to our families, "Children obey your parents in the Lord, for this is right. Honor your father and your mother, which is the first commandment of promise, that it may be well with you, and that ye may live long on the earth." If things can be well with me, because I have honored my parents, then obviously God must be the source of this stability and security. Are you getting excited, yet?

Continued financial insufficiency--- Deuteronomy 28:17, 29, 47-48, "Cursed shall be your kneading bowl ... you shall not prosper in your ways ... because you did not serve the Lord your God with joy and gladness of heart, for the abundance of all things; therefore, you shall serve your enemies, whom the Lord will send against you, in hunger, in thirst, in nakedness, and in need of all things ..."

In Matthew 12:36-37, we have the solemn warning from Jesus, "But I say to you that for every idle word men may speak, they will give account of it in the day of judgment. For by your words you will be justified, and by your words you will be condemned." I am here to confess, the Holy Spirit "pounded" me with this verse. I have let many "idle" words stream from my mouth. Let's take the five symptoms above and listen to ourselves momentarily:

Mental and Emotional disorders: "These kids are driving me crazy. I can't take it anymore."

Repeated or chronic sickness: "Whenever there is a bug around, I seem to catch it... Cancer seems to run in the family, I guess, I'm next ..."

Barrenness, Female Problems: "I don't think I will ever get pregnant." "I've got the curse again (monthly cycle)."

Breakdown of Marriage and Family: "You never did love me", "Our family can't get together without some type of conflict."

Continual Financial Problems: "I don't know where the money goes." "I can't afford to tithe"

There are various moral and ethical sins that can cause curses. In Deuteronomy 27:15-26 there are twelve moral and ethical sins mentioned all of which can provoke God's curse. I would suggest that you study these carefully and allow the Holy Spirit to illuminate you. The following is a suggested summary of the main ideas covered by them: acknowledging and worshiping false gods, disrespect for parents, all forms of oppression and injustice especially when directed against the weak and helpless, and all forms of illicit or unnatural sex.

And let's remember that Satan can work through our curses. We have already suggested that Satan's plan is to "steal our joy, kill our spirit, and destroy our souls and bodies (John 10:10). Ephesians 6:12 makes it clear that we "wrestle not against flesh and blood but against principalities and powers: against spiritual wickedness in high places." Dearly beloved, let me say the obvious: When we are arguing, when those words are flowing from our mouths, this sets in motion effects beyond our comprehension. We are reinforcing our own sickness; we are allowing Satan to get "footholds" in our lives, and we are potentially affecting our children and grandchildren and great grandchildren.

God does desire to bless us. In Malachi 3:8-9 it relates that if we "bring all our tithes into the storehouse, that there may be food in my house, and prove me now in this. Says the Lord of hosts ... I will open for you the windows of heaven and pour out for you such blessings that there will not be enough room to receive it." Praise God he relates that if we "draw nigh to Him that He will draw nigh to us (James 4:8), and if we turn to His reproof that He will pour out His Spirit unto us, and will make known His words unto us (Proverbs 1:23)". Praise the

Lord. Will you take all of that He will give you? And, of course, we have the "beatitudes" in Matthew 5:3¬11. He wants us to be "poor in spirit (humble), to be meek, and to be merciful, and to be sympathetic, and to be determined, and be pure, and to be peaceable ... and the results will be that we "will be filled, obtain mercy, inherit the earth, and see God."

This material is about to turn from the pessimistic to the optimistic. The last part of this book will deal with the healing process. Let's close this chapter by turning our curses into blessings. James 4:7 promises that if we "resist the devil he will flee from us." Such a promise... But change is dependent on our wills, our volition. We have to have the determination that we are going to conquer our anger and our argumentative spirit.

We have the potential for a new Covenant. Hebrews 10:4 states, "For by one offering He hath perfection forever for them that are sanctified ... This is the covenant that I will make with them after those days, saith the Lord, I will put my laws into their hearts and minds ..." Ah folks, how would you like the Lord to put His laws into your hearts and minds? Let me suggest five steps in moving our curses to blessings.

Step One – Realization: Carl Jung was correct, "self realization is the first step of change." In Proverbs 24:32, after presenting the imagery of a "broken down" house, Solomon presents this scenario of change, "Then I saw (realization), and considered it (reflection), and looked upon it (identification), and received instruction (change). I would suggest that there are two parts of this first step.

(1) We must identify the curse. Let's take the three passages of Scripture that deal with flesh and lump them together (Galatians 5:19-21, Mark 7:21-22, and Ephesians 5:31). "... bitterness, wrath, anger, clamor (confusion), evil speaking, malice (getting back) ... evil thoughts, adulteries, fornications, murders, thefts, covetousness, wickedness, deceit, lasciviousness (lust), evil eye, blasphemy, pride, foolishness ... adultery, uncleanness (sexual things), idolatry, witchcraft, hatred, variance (person against person), emulations (jealousies), wrath, strife, sedition's, heresies, envying, murders, drunkenness, and revellings ..." Let's take three of these that might be prevalent in your life. Are anger and wrath among them?

(2) We must identify the source. Do you know of others within your extended family that manifests any of these characteristics?

Step Two - Repentance: Repentance is a prerequisite for God's mercy and grace. Let's not forget that awesome passage in Isaiah 53:4-5, "Surely He hath borne our griefs and carried our sorrows, yet we did esteem him stricken, smitten of God and afflicted. He was wounded for our transgressions, He was bruised for our iniquities, the chastisement of our peace was upon Him, and with His stripes we are healed." You heard it, didn't you? We have the potential to be healed. Jesus did this for you and for me. We have two steps here. We must confess our desire to have this curse and sin removed from us. 1 John 1:9 says, "If we confess our sins, He is faithful and just to forgive us our sins, and to cleanse us from all unrighteousness." And we must receive the remission. John 16:23-24, "Whatsoever ye shall ask the Father in my name, He will give it you. Hitherto have ye asked nothing in my name, ask, and ye shall receive, that your joy may be full."

Step Three – Release. 1 Peter 5:7 says, "Casting (releasing) all your cares upon Him, for He careth for you." Praise God the time has come for a releasing of our curses. I would encourage all of us to repeat this prayer (taken from Derek Prince's book).

"Lord Jesus Christ, I believe that You are the Son of God and the only way to God, and that You died on the cross for my sins and rose again from the dead. I give up all my rebellion and all my sin, and I submit myself to You as my Lord. I confess all my sins before You and ask for Your forgiveness, especially for any sins that exposed me to a curse. Release me from the consequences of my ancestors' sins. By a decision of my will, I forgive all that have harmed me or have wronged me---just as I want you Father to forgive me. In particular I forgive ... (list of people)

I renounce all contacts with anything occult or satanic. If I have any "contact objects", I commit myself to destroy them. I cancel all Satan's claims against me. I pray Lord that I may be released from any "footholds" in my body, soul, or spirit that the devil has upon me, and in Jesus name... in Jesus name... I pray for release of any evil spirits that might presently control me. Lord Jesus, I believe that on the cross You took on Yourself every curse that could ever come upon me. So I ask

You now to release me from every curse over my life --- in your name, Lord Jesus Christ. By faith I now receive my release and my blessings. Thank you for peace. Thank you for release in Jesus name."

Step Four --- Reconciliation. Many folks know 11 Corinthians 5:17, "Therefore if any man be in Christ, he is a new creature, old things are passed away; behold all things are become new." But the passage continues in verse 18 to relate that He has given unto us the "ministry of reconciliation." Two verses further says that He will give unto us the very "words of reconciliation." The word reconciliation literally means, "closing the gap ...". It is our job to close the gap with anyone to whom we are estranged. We first must identify those with whom we need to be reconciled. Secondly, we have to cross over into their world. The apostle Paul said that he "became all things to all men that by some means, he might win some". It is our task to remake the person in our minds. As Lewis Smedes stated in his book *Forgive and Forget*, ". . . we remake the person . . . in our minds, we look to them now not as the person who hurt us, but the person who needs us." Gaps are not always closed, but we do have the power to remake that person in our minds.

If you have followed these steps, praise His Holy name, God has renewed you. Romans 12:2 states that we can be "transformed by the renewing of our mind" Let's believe that God has affirmed a "new covenant" within you (Hebrews 10:14-16). Let's believe that God has given to you a new "inner strengthening." Ephesians 3: 16 states, "That He would grant you according to the riches of His glory to be strengthened with might by His Spirit in the inner man." God wants to turn your "curses to blessings". Proverbs 8: 17-21 says, "I love them that love me, and those that seek me early shall find me. Riches and honor are with me, yea, durable riches and righteousness. My fruit is better than gold, yea, than fine gold; and my revenue than choice silver. I lead in the way of righteousness, in the midst of the paths of judgment. That I may cause those that love me to inherit substance, and I will fill their treasures." God desires to do so much within our lives.

I trust all of you, who are struggling with an argumentative spirit, have worked to apply this chapter. I will give some depth considerations to our emotions in the next chapter, and then there will be three chapters dealing with the healing of the argumentative spirit. The best is yet to come.

7

The Expressions of an Argument

The battle is real. The consequences are real. The sickness is real. The healing of anger must involve understanding the functioning of the spirit and the soul. We do have options as to how we respond to a given stimulus. Thus, the will becomes a strong factor in this "triggering" mechanism.

The assumption throughout this book is that anger and argumentation is correlated. I suppose that we have all had discussions with people that were entirely rational. Feelings were not involved. Argumentation generally becomes the foundation for anger. Thus, it must be addressed. Argumentation is the initiation; anger is "full blown". Argumentation is the triggering; anger is the expression. An argument is responding incorrectly to an issue; anger is expressing it. I grant you that it is difficult at times to know the "inner man" of a person. Let's raise a controversy. In Matthew 21:13, when Jesus "went into the temple of God, and cast out all them that sold and bought in the temple, and overthrew the tables of the money-changers, and the seats of them that sold doves". Was He angry? I think not. You might retort, "Wait a minute. He is turning over tables." That is true, but we don't know what He is feeling. In graduate school, I learned about an "objective reaction". I could presume a certain "persona", when in fact I was very rational. There were times with my kids that I would raise my voice and say with great authority, "Clean up that mess right now." Did the kids think I was angry? Yes. Was I? Generally, I was not. This was entirely objective; this was entirely for effect. I think Jesus realized that if He had said, "Please guys, pretty please, don't make my Father's house a den of thieves", he would not have had their attention. They got His point. I think He was totally "rational" inwardly.

Now, conversely, there were many other times that I was both angry and argumentative. My kids are grown, but I have been reminded that one of the best "arguments" between my wife and I occurred in a car traveling from Ann Arbor to Traverse City, Michigan. This is a four and half-hour trip, and we must have "occupied" at least two hours of it with harsh words. I was so dumb, and I was so sick.

Basically, we judge others by their words. We have an entire chapter in James 3 dealing with the tongue. Verse 10 relates that out of the same mouth proceedeth blessing and cursing. "My brethren, these things ought not so to be." The passage continues to challenge us that if we are wise and have knowledge, it will be emulated through our "conversation and meekness" (verse 13). Interestingly, both verses 14 and 16 warn us of having "envying and strife" within us. That inner "strife" affects our tongues.

Matthew 12:36 warns us that ultimately, we will be judged by God through our words, "But I say unto you, that every idle word that man shall speak, they shall give account thereof in the day of judgment." That is sobering. But Proverbs 25:11 relates that a "word fitly spoken is like apples of gold and pictures of silver." My mother used to have her hair done on Fridays, and inevitably, she would return home "fluffing" her hair (she was great), and say, "How do I look?" The next words from my mouth were crucial. "Mom," I would say, "You look____" (A word fitly spoken).

We have basically, eight emotions. There are love, joy, sorrow, anger, fear, anxiety, jealousy and hate. Thus, within our discussion of "Stress Anthropology" anger is one of our emotions, and our emotions are within our soul. In the development of our anger there are two variables: (1) development and (2) capacity. No two individuals have the same capacity for each emotion, and no two individuals have the same environment as to development. As has been discussed, because I had a background of anger, it was easier for this to be expressed.

Our society directly promotes this illness. Consider with me sports like boxing, and wrestling, and soccer, and football. They promote violence. I played football both in high school and college. When I had a blocking assignment, where my task was to "hit" this man as hard as I could, was this not reinforcing anger? And literarily, millions of fans vicariously do the same as spectators. How many times have we yelled, "Kill the umpire?" And think of the consequences emotionally of violence in video games, movies, and television. Can we imagine a society where all that is removed? Can we imagine a society where we play sports, but we don't keep score? As of this writing, we have soldiers who have been asked to go to war. Are we surprised that they return home and are violent to their spouses or children? I am aware that freedom must be defended; but the toll is paid many times off the battlefield.

What does God want to happen to our emotions? Let's consider three passages: 1. Thessalonians 3: 12, "And the Lord make you to increase and abound in love one toward another". John 15:11, "These things I have spoken unto you that my joy might remain in you, and that your joy might be full." And finally, Ephesians 4:29-32, "Let no needless communications proceed out of your mouth (get a handle on that thought), but that which is good for the use of edifying, that it may minister grace to the hearers. And grieve not the Holy Spirit of God, whereby ye are sealed unto the day of redemption. Let all bitterness and wrath, and anger, and clamor, and evil speaking by put away from you (that's our goal) with no malice. And be kind to one another, tenderhearted, forgiving one another, even as God for Christ's sake has forgiven you." It would be good for all of us to stop and reflect on these passages momentarily.

Arguments are defined as a "strong discussion between two individuals" and anger as "when ideas become self-willed." However, I ask you, the last time you got into an argument, how open were you to the other's view? Let's suppose for the sake of discussion, that this argument has become "heated" enough that you are now under attack. If your spouse is reminding you "how stupid" your thinking might be, my guess would be that you are not thinking, "Yes, please tell me more." No, you are probably thinking, "As soon as they slow down", I am going to remind them of their idiosyncrasies."

The premise of an argument is simple. If I talk long enough, or loud enough, or direct enough, I will persuade my spouse to change his/her mind. Now come on. It took me years to understand that when I am arguing with my wife, I am forcing her to defend an issue that I believe to be wrong. It becomes counter-productive because she is reinforcing her beliefs with every word. From this, we get the insight as to why people argue more than once over the same issue. And tragically sometimes, this continues for years. Provocative, right? Sick people argue. Healthy people can be quiet. Proverbs 17:27, "He that hath knowledge spares his words; and a man of understanding is of an excellent spirit." The only way you can change people is to love them.

CONE OF ARGUMENT

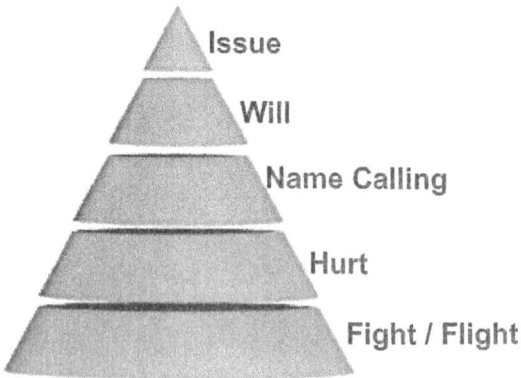

I call it the "Cone of Argumentation." These are the steps of an argument. After reading this material, if you are ever tempted to "argue" again, you will be able to identify exactly where you are.

Now you would think that rational people could resolve their differences on an issue level. If you apply this to international problems, you would think (as an example) that Palestine and Israel would realize that sitting down and resolving their differences issue by issue is more provocative than "suicide bombings" or "running tanks" through the West Bank. Again, sickness breeds sickness. Wounded and crushed spirits become contagious, and finally it spreads.

Then it becomes will against will. If I give in to her, I will become "hen pecked." Who does he think he is? This is an era of women's rights. If it leaves the "issue phase," everything "ill tempered" can be triggered. I recall attempting to put my will against my father when I was young. As I recall, I suggested that he "shut up." I have never seen a man get excited so quickly.

This leads to name-calling and hurt. Even if you have not directly attacked through name-calling, have you ever implied such? If we say, "That is a dumb idea ... that notion is so stupid." Since you are the person behind the idea or notion, the implication is obvious. And the hurt can take either a physical and/or mental dimension. There can be physical or verbal abuse. If you are not aware, with the exception of motor car violations, domestic violence is the number one problem of police work. I know a former state policeman, who was injured once in his years of service. He was hit in the shoulder by a knife thrown by a wife at her husband.

Finally, there is fight or flight. Let's ask it forthrightly. Have you ever hit your spouse? Have the police ever been called to your home for domestic violence? Many couples engage in silence or flight. They separate or close their spirits to one another. This is the "chafed" person (also a sign of sickness). I remember two situations. In one, I arrived at the house to intercede with an arguing couple. He had his bags packed, and he was going home to mother (which he did). In the other situation, the husband had been unfaithful to his wife. When I arrived, he was in the yard, and we chatted for a while. He gave permission for me to go into the house. As I entered the house, a plate came flying over my head. The wife was so "angry" with her husband, that she was ready to hit him with a plate when he walked through the door. Fortunately, for me she was both a "poor shot" and a very apologetic person.

An argument and anger can escalate to rage, resentment, and indignation. Rage is violent and explosive and manifested outwardly. Resentment is rage turned inside. It is repressed feelings of anger that usually smolder and seek revenge. Indignation (justice) is controlled feelings of justice. Note that indignation has a rational base. From his excellent book Anger, *Yours and Mine and What to Do about it*, Richard Walters makes these comparisons:

1.   Rage seeks to do wrong. Resentment seeks to hide wrong. Indignation seeks to correct wrongs.

2.   Rage and resentment seek to destroy people. Indignation seeks to destroy evil.

3.   Rage and resentment seek vengeance. Indignation seeks justice.

4.   Rage is guided by selfishness. Resentment is guided by cowardice. Indignation is guided by mercy.

5.   Rage uses open warfare. Resentment is a guerilla fighter. Indignation is an honest, fearless, forceful, defender of truth.

6.   Rage defends itself. Resentment defends the status quo. Indignation defends the other person.

The Expressions of an Argument

7.   Rage and resentment are forbidden in the Bible. Indignation is encouraged.

There are basically three Greek words for anger in the New Testament. Each one conveys a different "expression" of anger.

(1) Anger as defined by "tumos." This is a turbulent, boiling, agitation of feelings. It blazes up like a sudden explosion, and then it quickly subsides. We get our word tumult from this word. It is much like a match that blazes quickly and then subsides. It is mentioned some twenty times in the New Testament. Many times it is translated as the word "wrath." Ephesians 4:31, "Let all bitterness, and wrath (thumas), and anger be put away from you." Galatians 5:19-20, "Now the fruits of the flesh are manifest which are these: adultery, fornication, uncleanness, lasciviousness, idolatry, witchcraft, hatred, variance, emulations, wrath (tumas), and strife. "A wounded or crushed individual, who has become ill-tempered, can easily develop an argumentative spirit. Because the spirit is fractured, it is easy for that individual to "go off the handle" and to express himself through strife and wrath. Proverbs 17: 1 states, "Better is a dry morsel and quietness therewith, than a house full of sacrifices and strife." You can serve steak dinners, but if there is anger and strife in your home, you will never have a healthy family.

(2) Anger as defined by "orge." This has the connotation of a settled, long lasting attitude. The person "internalizes" the anger. They are usually reflective and bent upon hurting back. "Orge" could be likened to coals slowly warming up to red,

91

then to white, and staying hot while holding a high temperature. This word is in the New Testament some forty five times. It is translated both anger and wrath. Ephesians 4:31 states, "let all bitterness, and wrath, and anger (orge) be put away from you." Romans 12:19-20, "Dearly beloved, avenge not yourselves, nor give place unto wrath (orge), for it is written, vengeance is mine, I will repay saith the Lord. Therefore if thine enemy hunger, feed him: if he is thirsty, give him drink. For in so doing thou shalt heap coals of fire of fire on his head." I call these people "scorekeepers." They are thinking, "You think I don't know what is happening, but I do. Someday, you will want something from me, and the answer is already no." Within marriage many times, money and sex become obvious weapons. The first group (tumos) is generally reactionary individuals; the orge people are more reflective.

(3) Anger as defined by "parorgismos." This is an anger that has been provoked. It is used three times in the New Testament. Ephesians 6:4, "Fathers provoke (parorgismos) not your children to wrath (parorgismos), but nurture them in the fear and admonition of the Lord." The interchange here is interesting. If I have an attitude of strife, I can drive forth strife and anger from my children. In teaching "*Marriage & Family*" classes, I have asked the students, "Were you ever slapped in the face?" Many of them cannot only relive the circumstances, but they can tell me what day of the week it was. They were provoked. They perhaps deserved discipline, but they did not deserve to be slapped in the face. In all candor, this expression is the most difficult for me. If I am "minding my own business" and

someone wants to provoke me, I have to be careful not to respond accordingly. After a recent conference, I started home only to have a "young buck" come up against my bumper from behind. The speed limit was 50 MPH on a two-lane highway. I was going 50, but we wanted to go 90. The sick part of me said, "Well, if you don't like 50, let's try 40 ... I had been provoked." The healthy side of me said, "Pull over and let him pass, which I did." As I was parked along the highway, I thought, "Twenty years ago, the outcome would have been much different."

8

Healing the Spirit – The Process

These next three chapters applied can not only stop all domestic problems, but they can impact murders and wars. Eventually, our prisons could be emptied. These next words are very important.

Biblically, there are two ways that people can change. **They can change through "renewal" and "restoration."** David in pleading before the Lord in Psalm 51, after his sin with Bathsheba, cried, "Create in me a clean heart, O God, and renew a right spirit within me. Cast me not away from thy presence, and take not thy Holy Spirit from me." David came before the Lord with a repentant heart. If only that would be our starting point, if only we would desire to rid ourselves of any sin, God would honor it. Who has been hurt through your anger? After you come before the Lord, make a list of individuals to whom you need to apologize. Note that David was concerned about the Lord taking his Holy Spirit from him. In Romans 1:29 God gives individuals over to a "reprobate mind." Our stubbornness and lack of contriteness keeps us from knowing the blessings of God in our lives. Note, however, that David desired to be "renewed." "Renew a right spirit within me." This word renew is mentioned throughout Scripture. In Isaiah 40:31, those that "wait upon the Lord can have their strength renewed." Romans 12:2, "challenges us to not be conformed to this world, but be ye transformed by the renewing of your mind" The Greek and Hebrew words for "renew" connote thoughts like "rebuilding" or "renovating". I like the thought set forth in one of the commentaries of being "better than new." How would you like to drive your car for 200,000 miles, and one day you walk outside, and it has been renewed. The car is better than new. Praise God, it is not where we have been, it is where we are going. Brace yourself for a real renewal.

Obviously, however, if we are sick from erethism, and if we have a fractured spirit, we initially need a healing within our spirits. It is intriguing that since anger is one of our emotions, and since in this culture, the "heart" was considered the "emotional center" of the individual, that David's plea included a real cleansing of his emotions. Among the possible translations of the word "right" in our passage (right spirit), is the word perfect or correct. God desires to renew us. God is striving to draw from us holiness, righteousness, and perfection (Matthew 5:48, Ephesians 4:24).

Imagine with me a new society. In this society we not only have clinics for the healing of physical and mental disorders, we have clinics for the healing of emotional disorders. Many years ago, I began counseling a young man, who was eventually incarcerated on a second-degree murder charge. He became angry over "homosexual advances" by an older man, and he bludgeoned this man to death with a knife and a rifle barrel. I committed myself to visiting him during his imprisonment. In one of my first sessions, I made an appointment to visit his counselor. After some discussion concerning my counseling of him, I inquired how he would be helping him. His remarks are fixated in my mind, "Do you think I am a counselor; I am a paper pusher. I am responsible for 168 men. I don't have time to personally counsel them individually." Our society is so prone to deal with the effect and not the cause. In the society that I want to create, when any anger or rage is manifested, the individual and family must get emotional help. Among the purposes of this clinic is a "renewal" of their spirits. The purpose in part of these clinics is to totally "rebuild" and "renovate" the very "essence of life" within the individual, his spirit.

We have dissipated so much. Would it not be better to "rebuild" the lives of our prison inmates emotionally?

We also must not only "renew" the spirit; we must "restore" the soul. Let's remember that the soul is the interpretive part of our personality. David in Psalm 51 asks of God to "restore unto me the joy of thy salvation ... " The 23rd Psalm begins, "The Lord is my shepherd; I shall not want. He maketh me to lie down in green pastures; he leadeth me beside the still waters, He restoreth my soul. The Hebrew word for restore is "sheva" or a returning to the starting point. I sometimes ask couples during counseling, "When was the happiest time in your marriage?" Now for the healthy couple, the correct answer should be today. But many of the couples struggle to think back to a happier time. The passage communicates that all of us are "in a state of flux." There is no "status quo" anything. You are either happier or sadder today than you were yesterday. You are either more or less spiritual today than you were yesterday. And yes ... you are either more or less angry today than you were yesterday. Probably, in a war setting, anger will dissipate to rage. The dissipation will continue until the "conscience is seared", and a man will be able to kill with no feelings of remorse. Just this day, I heard on the radio where Palestinian soldiers arrested a Palestinian woman. She was accused of abetting the enemy. They took her to another building, and shot her. My guess would be that the Palestinian soldier will not lose any sleep tonight. Or think of a Timothy McVee who bombed the Federal Building in Oklahoma City. He probably believed right to his death, that he was right and everyone else was wrong. I would surmise that he gave little thought to the many innocent lives that were lost.

Before we walk through the steps of healing, let's consider that "triggering mechanism within the spirit." It takes little for the triggering to occur. "Honey, would you take out the garbage?", the wife asked. That seems an innocent enough request. But I can think of a couple, whom I counseled, that the taking out of the garbage became the battlefield. She wanted him daily to take out the garbage. He resisted. She would leave the bag by the back door. He resisted. She would leave it on the walk to the car. He would walk by it. Finally, one night he came home late. He noticed on the way in that the garbage was gone. He assumed that he had won. They had twin beds, and that night as he got into bed, it was filled with garbage. Something very small had become something very large.

What do you feel when you are belittled? What do you feel when your spouse verbally attacks you? Again, that triggering mechanism becomes everything.

(1) **There is ignition.** Ecclesiastes 7:9 states, "Be not hasty in thy spirit to be angry; for anger resteth in the bosom of fools." The Hebrew word for "hasty" means to "tremble inwardly, or to be agitated." The first thing that I must understand is this "triggering mechanism" is that there is a spark, an ignition. I must become conscious of it.. Thinking in terms of this "triggering mechanism", to me the strongest "integration" passage in the Scriptures is the Sermon on the Mount (Matthew 5 – 7). Imagine the teaching of Jesus when he said "agree with thine adversary quickly ... (Matthew 5:25). "If someone "smites thee on thy right cheek, turn to him the other also (5:39)." Before continuing, are you observing a new way of thinking? In Matthew 5:41, Jesus continues, "And whosoever shall compel thee to go a mile, go with him two ... " I heard a speaker many years ago expound on this thought. He related that the Jewish people were under bondage to the Romans at this time. And

the Romans had passed a law that if a soldier "demanded" a Jewish citizen to carry his "goods" a mile, he or she had to comply. Jesus was now saying, "Don't carry the goods one mile, carry them two miles." Can you imagine ... can you imagine? Let's presume that we lost the war in Afghanistan, and we were in bondage to the Taliban. Let's presume that they had this type law in place. What would be going through your spirit and soul as you carried their goods? And let's imagine that a "religious leader" advocated that I don't carry the goods one-mile, but that I carry them two miles. What would be your human response to him? As the speaker expounded in a college chapel, "For the first mile you would be under Roman submission because you are following a law, but for the second mile the Roman soldier would be under submission to you, because you are doing it willfully."

In considering the establishing of constructs within the person (their way of doing something) , obviously, people deal with these tensions subconsciously differently.

There is the denier. This person represses it. He chooses to deal with it by not dealing with it. This is the non-confrontational person. Besides the "internalization" process, he becomes emotionally padded to it.

There is the stuffer. This person suppresses it. He does personalize it, but he also holds it in. This is the "orge" anger. He becomes a scorekeeper. He will look for opportunities for revenge.

There is the yeller. The person expresses it. This is the "tumos" or "parorgismos" anger. This is the "scoffer" in Proverbs 9. This is the individual who "makes with the mouth". It generally takes little to ignite the spirit.

There is the processor. The person confesses it. This is the goal of these last chapters. The three mechanisms of the first three are emotional, but to become a processor, an individual must be led by the rational over the emotional.

(2) There is volition. James 4: 1-5 states, "From whence come wars and fighting among you, come they not hence, even of your lusts that war in your members. Your lust, and have not, you kill and desire to have and cannot obtain, you fight and war, yet you have not ... the spirit that dwelleth in us lusteth to envy." Wars are not fought over land or philosophy, they are fought over pride and greed. Our proof text in Proverbs 16:32, "says he that is slow to anger is better than the mighty, and he that rules his spirit can take a city." How do you rule your spirit? It is not easy. At the moment of the stimulus, during the ignition phase, I decide by volition that my response will not be one of anger. The greatest psychological passage in all of Holy Writ (I do believe it) is found in Mark 7:14-23. Jesus in verse 14 calls the people to Himself and pleads for them to "understand." He then teaches, "there is nothing from without a man that entering into him can defile him, but the things which come out of him, those are they that defile him." When the disciples were left alone with him in verse 18 they asked him the meaning. Jesus says, "Are you also without understanding? Do you not perceive that whatsoever thing from without enters into the man cannot defile him ... because it enters not into the heart (our emotions, our will, etc)? He then describes the process of the "elimination" of foods to the disciples. (I love it when Jesus has a sense of humor). Then in verse 21, he concludes, "For from within, out of the heart of men, proceed evil thoughts, adulteries, fornications, murders, thefts, covetousness, wickedness, deceit, lasciviousness, and evil eye, blasphemy, pride, foolishness. All these things come from within and defile the man." Do you get His point? Anything expressed outwardly must start inwardly. It is not what happens to me, it is how I interpret what happens to me. No person, no situation, no circumstance is any more of a threat to me than I make it. Our will becomes the key.

Let's practice. Your child has just told you to "shut up." What is your response? Remember it starts with ignition and volition. I have many options both as what I feel and how I respond. Your husband has just told you that you are "getting fat." What is your response? Remember it starts with ignition and volition. Your wife has just made clear that there will be no sex tonight. What is your response? Remember it starts with ignition and volition.

(3) Lastly, there is sanctification. The process of Satan is obvious. He utilizes the world to activate my flesh, which stems from a sin nature that is set for me to be in rebellion. Since I am "trans-generationally" prone to anger, it is easy for me to express it, and the devil gets a foothold in my life. Thus, when I am into my fifteenth argument with my wife, over some "dumb" things, I don't even think of the possibility of being a sick man. But if you recall in chapter one, we discussed "Stress Anthropology." We defended the idea that "whatever the tension, it must have a source." What is the source of flesh and sin within me? If I basically have spirit, soul, and body (I Thessalonians 5:23), from which of these sources is flesh? The strongest evidence is that "flesh" and "sin" starts from my spirit. Galatians 5: 17 relates that, "the flesh lusteth (or wars) against the Spirit, and the Spirit against the flesh." If we review the fruits of the flesh: "adultery, fornication, uncleanness, lasciviousness (lust), idolatry, witchcraft, hatred, variance emulations, wrath, strife, seditions, heresies, envying, murders, drunkenness, reveling, and the likes, . . ." It is obvious that my soul is involved since all these qualities have "interpretative" features, but there has to also be that "triggering" mechanism that indicates that my spirit is involved.

Now conversely, a righteous God desires to change you and me. Theologically, we call this sanctification. If we take our proof verse I Thessalonians 5:23, it states, "May the God of peace sanctify you wholly, and I pray God your whole spirit, soul, and body be preserved blameless". Let those words ring in our ears. He wants to "sanctify us wholly." The Greek words here relate that God desires to "absolutely fill us with holiness and purity." Let's correlate this to our discussion of an argumentative spirit. Let's explore three goals in this sanctifying process.

(I) Sanctification --- God desires to destroy the flesh. In Galatians 5: 16, in the discussion of the dynamics of the Holy Spirit in a believer's life, it relates in verse 24 that "they that are Christ's have crucified the flesh with the affections and lusts." And can you imagine implementing verse 26, "Let us not be desirous of vain glory, provoking one another, envying one another." Praise God. That is us. You can't remember the last time that you "provoked" someone or someone "provoked" you. This is after the challenge in verse 25 that if "we live in the Spirit, let us also walk in the Spirit." Which is a good King James's way of saying if "you preach it, practice it." Or what of Romans 6:2 that states, "God forbid, How shall we, that are dead to sin, live any longer therein?" Isn't it nice folks to be "dead to sin." Boy, I can't remember the last time that I had a sinful thought? Can you? (You understand that I am being facetious). And if we go on with the passage, it doesn't get any better. Romans 6:6-7 states, "Knowing this, that our old man is crucified with him, that the body of sin might be destroyed, that henceforth we should not serve sin. For he that is dead is freed from sin". God not only wants to free you from an argumentative spirit, He wants to free you from the very source of that anger and argumentation, your flesh and sin nature.

(2) Sanctification --- God wants to move us from law to grace. I must confess that I never understood this discussion of law and grace from Romans 6-8. One day, the Holy Spirit hit me with the truth (for me), and I was knocked out of my socks. The passage begins in Romans 6:1 with the question whether we "should continue in sin that grace may abound?" He answers his own question by saying, "God forbid". God gave to us the "law" or His commandments because we were dumb. To some of us it created "legalism", or we became preoccupied with people living by a set of rules. We become judgmental and frustrated. In Romans 7:22, Paul states that he delights in the law in the inward man, but then he goes on to discuss the battle within his mind of not being able to follow the law, or these rules. There is a segment within all religions that battle this. I must bow to Mecca. I must go to all the services at church. Then we go home and argue with our wives. Something is missing. Get ready to hold on to something. In Romans 7:7 it takes us a step further, "What shall we say then? Is the law sin? God forbid. Nay, I had not known sin, but by the law, for I had not known lust, except the law had said. Thou shalt not covet." Do we get it? We are so dumb that God had to establish laws for our conduct. He had to establish laws, because we are so dumb that we would destroy ourselves. Hello. Wait a minute. In certain circles we are doing exactly that now. In the name of religion, Moslem terrorists on September 11, 2001, piloted planes in the World Trade Center in New York City and killed some 3000 people. They were in bondage. They were under "the law." But this same rationale is true for the person in bondage to an argumentative spirit. Our conscious mind can be "seared" and there is little guilt, but to others of us, after "massive arguments", we are saying that "we are sorry". Now what God is striving to do for us is to move us from law to grace. Let Romans 8:2 ring in our ears, "For the law of the Spirit of life in Christ Jesus hath made me free ... that's free ... from the law of sin and death." God wants to free us from ourselves and move us to grace. Let me illustrate. If I believe my wife, when I was a young man I had a bit of a "heavy foot" while driving. There was a time or two that the "law" reminded me that she was correct. Now ... much older, I drive the Detroit freeways to get to the college. The speed limit is 70 miles per hour, and I am generally under that on the inside lane. My point is that they can post any speed limit they want. I have moved from "law to grace." I drive the speed limit, now not because I have to, but because I want to. It is amazing isn't it? My point is that as you progress through sanctification, you will discover a complete metamorphosis in your argumentative spirit. You will say within yourself, I can't believe that this type statement at one point "duped" me into an argument.

(3) Sanctification --- Moving from contention to meekness and humility. God's goal for argumentative people is meekness and humility. I said, "God's goal for argumentative people is meekness and humility." Let me shout it, "GOD'S GOAL FOR ARGUMENTATIVE PEOPLE IS MEEKNESS AND HUMILITY."

Humility, I like to define as "understanding who we are in relationship to whom God is". Imagine how our space program is viewed from God's perspective. Assume for a moment that God is the creator of the universe. He put the sun and stars in place. And then one day, he observes this little "metal can" headed for one of the moons that He created. It makes little difference how many years you have been to college or how many books you have read. Compared to God, we "know nothing about nothing." But it is more than that. It is what the person really is. He is "lowly". He "esteems others better than Himself." He is a servant to others. How much would you have to change to become lowly? James 4:10 states that if we "humble ourselves in the sight of the Lord, He will lift us up." The opposite of humility is pride. It has been said that the reason God is hard on proud people is because "pride is taking on God-like qualities ... "We think that we are all knowing, etc... James 4:6 relates that "God resisteth the proud and giveth grace to the humble." Proverbs 22:4 says that "by humility and fear of the Lord are riches, and honor, and life." How would you like to have riches and honor and life? Well your task is easy, you just have to become humble and develop an awesome "reverence for God."

Meekness has been described as "quiet power. . .I know that I am right; so why get excited." But it is stronger than that. The original word means "mild." How much would we have to change to become mild? Meekness, not anger is triggered during stress. We have moved from being "high strung" to easy going. I had a "father in law" that was indeed a meek man. I don't recall ever seeing him express anger. He never got into an argument. He would state his opinion and he was done. Do we understand the strength of Jesus' words in Matthew 11 :28-30, "Come unto me all you that labor and are heavy laden, and I will give you rest. Take my yoke upon you and learn of me, for I am meek and lowly in heart, and you shall find rest unto your souls. For my yoke is easy, and my burden is light." God desires for us to have rest in our souls. God desires us to become mild. The strongest passage that correlates this anti-thesis between contention and meekness is James 3:13-17. Hold on to this. This is a dynamic truth. "Who is a wise man and endued with knowledge among you? Let him shew out of a good conversation his works with meekness of wisdom (that's meekness of wisdom). But if ye have bitter envying and strife in your hearts, glory not, and lie not against the truth. This wisdom descendeth not from above, but is earthly, sensual, devilish (that's devilish). For where envying and strife is there is confusion (disorder) and every evil work. But the wisdom that is from above is first pure, then peaceable, gentle, and easy to be intreated, full of mercy and good fruits, without partiality, and without hypocrisy". Do you sense the "sanctifying" process? Do you sense a righteous God, through the Holy Spirit, desiring to make some dynamic changes within you?

I think we are ready now to "grasp" the structure for change. Hold on.

9

Healing the Spirit - The Structure

Who corrects you? To whom do you go for counsel? Obviously, this chapter is crucial in our changing from contention to meekness, from pride to humility.

When someone is attempting to "change our minds", are we listening or are we thinking rebuttal. Bill Gothard relates that there are four different levels of friendship.

As he defines it, an acquaintance has the freedom to know someone on a name to name basis. How many people know that you are alive, and when they see you they know you by name? Think of a number. The second level is the casual friend. This is the freedom to have something in common with them. Think of a number. This would include people at work, school, church, etc. The third level is the close friend. With a close friend you have the freedom to share ideas and thoughts.

Again, think of a number. And finally, the last level is what he calls an intimate friend. This is someone who has the freedom to correct you, and you have the freedom to correct him or her. How many people do you know of this level? Think of a number. One of those often-overlooked passages is James 5:16, "Confess your faults one to another, and pray one for another, that ye may be healed" When was the last time you attended a service at your church where people were "confessing their faults one to another?" I have lived a few years, and I have never attended such a service. So the key to changing your argumentative spirit is a willingness to be corrected.

Let's go one step deeper. Proverbs 9:6-10 states, "Forsake the foolish and live, and go in the way of understanding. He that reproves a scorner gets to himself shame and he that rebukes a wicked man gets himself a blot. Reprove not a scorner, lest he hate thee; rebuke a wise man, and he will love thee. Give instruction to a wise man, and he will be yet wiser; teach a just man, and he will increase in learning. The fear of the Lord is the beginning of wisdom, and the knowledge of the holy is understanding." Please note the movement in verse six. We are moving from foolishness to life, and we are getting on the "way of understanding." How would you like to be one of the few people in the world who "understand" what is really happening? You will also note that there are three different people in the passage: (1) the wicked man, or the fighter, (2) the scorner, or the talker, and (3) the wise man, or the listener.

Let's ask ourselves, which one of these best characterizes us? Note that if you try to correct the wicked man, you will get a blot. This is a physical blemish. Why do people fight, or hit, or abuse others? Are they not striving to force their will on others? If you try and correct a scorner, he will attempt to shame you (put you down). A scorner will hate you. That's strong language. The scorner literally in Hebrew means, "one who makes with the mouth." This person has an opinion about everything. You can bring up any topic that you desire, and he will tell you where you are wrong. Finally, there is the wise man. " ... rebuke a wise man, and he will love you ..." That's us. As a wise person, do you want others to correct you? You seek counsel and correction, right?

I was studying this passage for a radio broadcast, when the Holy Spirit profoundly illuminated me. It struck me, "Duane, you are a scorner." In your teaching and counseling, you are giving "answers" continually. Who corrects you? You desire wisdom, but you are not willing to be corrected. I was hit decisively. That night when I went home, I said to my wife, "Honey, I want you to correct me." Well, after she hit the floor, and the shock subsided, she said, "You can't be serious." I related that I was very, very serious, and I shared how the Holy Spirit had convicted me. I promised that I would offer no rebuttal. Well, she began .... frankly .... and she talked ... and she talked. I thanked her, and then I went to two friends. Neither were "professional" people, but they were older and they knew me well. After they realized that I was serious, they said, well .... frankly. I related to one man, "If you had been

111

thinking these thoughts all of these years, why didn't you share them?" He related that you just don't go to others and say, "I think you would be a better person, if you would change the following qualities." I can relate that this experience was "life changing" for me. Well now .... are you ready to change? Are you ready to be corrected?

There are four steps in changing: (1) The Rational Phase --- all changes must start on a rational base. (2) The Revelation Phase --- what Biblical principles have been violated, (3) The Reinforcement Phase --- how do I inculcate these principles into my life? And (4) The Rebuilding Phase --- How do I get these truths into my heart and emotions? We will attempt to apply these steps in "removing" our argumentative spirit, but obviously, they can be applied to many other of our struggles.

(1) **The Rational Phase**--- Everyone has his or her own way of thinking. Let's speculate how differences in ideas have developed. I recall during the first year of our marriage, we "quarreled" over the toilet paper. I came from a home where the toilet paper was rolled under (the only correct way) and she came from a home where the toilet paper was rolled over (can you imagine?). When we visited the bathroom, we would turn the paper back and forth. Ridiculous, isn't it? Now you want to explain how your ideas were created and why you felt obligated to attempt to impose them on others?

In *Our Personality Theory* class at the college, we ask the students to give to us their favorite candy bar or their favorite color. Then I will challenge them, "How did that get to be your

112

favorite color or candy bar?" Few have an explanation. All of us have literally thousands of these "constructs." A construct is a set pattern of thinking. We have thousands built within us.

Let's explore again our proof text in Proverbs 16:32, "He that is slow to anger is better than the mighty, and he that rules his spirit than he that takes a city." Most argumentative people are neither "slow to anger" or do they "rule" their spirit. You obviously must start with a "rational consciousness" when the "ignition" occurs. This is difficult. Let's consider two other Scriptures. Proverbs 16:14 states, "The wrath of a king is as messengers of death, but a wise man will "pacify" it. Do you "irritate" tension, or do you "pacify" it. The word means to subdue or to bind.

Again, note the "rational consciousness." Your intent is not to instigate but to pacify. Your intent is not to make things worse, but your intent is to make them better. Proverbs 19:11 says, "The discretion of a man defers his anger, and it is his glory to pass over a transgression." The word "discretion" connotes that he "understands." He does not have to be drawn into an argument, because he knows what is "really going on." And the word "defer" means to "draw out" or "lengthen." Again, he is not one who immediately responds to situations. Most people with "argumentative" spirits have opinions and retort to almost anything.

So let's raise a few "rhetorical" questions:

Do I want to change?

Stop Arguing With Me

Do I understand that I have a problem?

Do I understand how my problem has affected others?

Am I willing to accept a new pattern (or construct) of thinking?

(2) **The Revelation Phase**--- We have moved into "rational consciousness", and now we want to know Biblically how our minds and thinking can be rebuilt. We all have our own perception of circumstances; so many times in counseling, I ask "patients" to imagine a third chair between the patients. I do relate that on chair one is his way of thinking, on chair two is her way of thinking, and on chair three is a Biblical way of thinking. Are we willing to follow the principles of chair number three? Are we willing to move from the "maladaptive" to the adaptive?

We have mentioned II Peter 1:4, "Whereby are given to us exceeding great and precious promises that we might be partakers of His Divine nature, having escaped the corruption in this world through lust." How would you like to become a partaker of His Divine nature? What a promise! God utilizes His Word to move us toward perfection, holiness, righteousness, and sanctification. We get there by inculcating "Biblical principles" (great and precious promises) into our lives. I contend that for any psychological and spiritual struggle, there is a Biblical solution.

We will cover this in the next chapter, but let's take one principle to water your taste. James 1:19-20 states, "Wherefore, my beloved brethren, let every man be swift to hear, slow to speak, slow to wrath: For the wrath of man worketh not the righteousness of God. This wrath of man is "orge", our scorekeeper. He internalizes and usually eventually expresses his anger. If you want to work against the will of God, be wrathful. The admonition is that we should be "slow to speak, slow to wrath (same word), and swift to hear." It hit me that we turn the admonitions in this verse around. Many of us are slow to hear, swift to speak, and swift to wrath. It has been said that God gave to us two ears and one mouth; so we could listen twice as much as we talk. Boy ... many of us do need to work on that principle.

Some rhetorical questions:

Do I understand my "maladaptive" instincts?

 Am I ready to become renewed?

Am I willing to conform to Biblical principles?

(3) **The Reinforcement Phase**--- How do we rebuild our constructs? How do we inculcate Biblical principles into our minds? One of my academic heroes was Paul Tournier. In his book *Understanding Ourselves* he related that if "we act how we want to feel, we will feel what we want to become (paraphrase)." When I read that I leaped. To me, it "screamed" truth, truth, and truth. When I was younger, I coined the phrase that "any of us can be a hypocrite until finally it becomes us." This was my way of saying that you set your goals mentally and give your emotions time to catch up. Eventually, these thoughts by Paul Tournier became known as the "fake it until you feel it

syndrome." Many disagreed with the concept. But for me it became the carrier for change. Whatever the Biblical principle, it must be lived, practiced, and reinforced, until finally the changes begin.

Let's review. My spirit was wounded and I became sick. It was affected by "interpretative" processes. At times, I was bitter and enraged. It carried over into my interpersonal relationships. The devil established a "foothold" in my life. But praise the Lord, I now rationally want to change. I am willing to conform to Biblical principles. I now know how to become this different person. I am going to take principles on controlling anger from God's word, and I am "going to fake it until I feel it." I am aware that initially I might not notice much change, but by keeping the "promises" (principles) constantly before me, it will eventually change my soul and spirit.

When I was a young man, I played basketball. I heard statements that "if you can shoot a jump shot, there will always be a place for you on the basketball team." Now what is being said is that the pretext of the game of basketball is to score points. If you can shoot a jump shot, and score points, they will want you on the team. I would like to bear witness that this is true. I used to practice shooting jump shots by the hour. This was emulated in one of the Chicago Bulls world championships. Of course, at that time, they had some "fairly" successful players like Scotty Pipen and Michael Jordan. But emblazed in my mind is the closing seconds of one of the final games. The Bulls were down by two points, and they called a "time out." Everyone assumed that they would build a play around Michael

Jordan. But they had a player called Johnny Paxton, who could basically do one thing. He could shoot a jump shot. They set a screen for him, and he released a three-point shot, hit it, and won the game. Can we speculate how many times he had "practiced" that shot? He, not Michael Jordan, was my hero. Do you want to change? It is easy. All you have to do is practice, practice, and practice. Jesus profoundly closed His sermon on the Mount in Matthew 7: 24 by saying, " . . . he that hears these sayings of mine and **puts them into practice**, I will liken to the wise man, who built his upon a rock . . ." There is the principle.

Many years ago, after a conference, a beautiful, elderly lady corrected me. During the session, I had made the statement that "practice makes perfect." She kindly corrected me. She related, "In due respect Dr. Cuthbertson, practice does not make perfect, practicing perfection makes perfect. "Wow!!! Is she right? With our argumentative spirit, many of us have practiced imperfection for years. Now the challenge is to conform our thinking to Biblical principle and practice, practice, practice ...

Some rhetorical questions:

Can you identify your bad habits?

Are you willing to begin applying Biblical principles to your life?

Are you willing to practice them?

(4) **The Rebuilding Phase**-- Remember change does not ensue until our feelings change. We think with our hearts. We are ultimately governed by our emotions. Proverbs 23:7 states, "For as he thinketh in his heart, so is he ..." John 14:21 is a favorite passage of mine. "He that has my commandments, and keeps them, he it is that loves me, and he that loves me shall be loved of my Father, and I will love him, and will manifest myself to him." How would you like to be loved by God, and to have Him manifest Himself to you? Amen. But note the correlation between our love for God and our keeping of His commandments. Our feelings ultimately must be changed. So in our alleviation of an argumentative spirit, it starts with the rational. It challenges us to know Biblical passages that relate to this topic, it stimulates us to reinforce those principles into our lives, until they finally hit our feelings and changes ensue.

I created this "Biblical Emotional Cycle." You will notice on the left is the regular "emotional cycle" and the "Biblical Emotional Cycle" is on the right.

Our regular cycle starts with arousal, to experience, to expression, and then to calm. Now applying that to anger: something is said that arouses us. This experience leads to an expression. Perhaps we even argue into the night. Finally, perhaps hours later, there is a calm.

Now, if we apply a Biblical theory to this cycle; note that after the arousal and experience, we move into a rational grid. We become determined to let our minds lead us and not our emotions. After we have activated the rational, we are now ready to apply Biblical principles to this arousal. What does the Bible say about this? Have I made a study at this point? Of course, this not only applies to an argumentative spirit, it applies to lust, depression, guilt, etc... Please note that the next step in this cycle is will. We have a sin nature. Have you ever done anything wrong, and while you were doing it, you knew that it was wrong, but you still decided to do it? So this structure has little value, unless you are motivated and determined to commit yourself to change. Now finally, within this cycle, you are ready for expression and calm.

And the Scriptures desire so much for us emotionally. As stated back in chapter seven, how would you like to be able to "rejoice in the Lord always (Phil.4:4), or have a joy that's full (John 15:11)? How you like to have a love that "abounds" (Philippians 1:9, I Thessalonians 3:12), or to be able to "rule" your spirit (Proverbs 16:32)? Praise God. Praise God.

10

Healing the Spirit – The Changed Person

Well, it has been an interesting journey. We have introduced you to "Stress Anthropology" and walked with you through the structure of man. We specifically analyzed man's spirit and soul. We defended indeed that there can be a "Healing an Argumentative Spirit". For argumentative people, their spirits have become fractured (erethism) as a result of being wounded or crushed. This leads many times to an interpretive soul of rage and bitterness, which tragically, Satan utilizes to get a "foothold" in our lives, and our struggles can become transgenerational.

Our desire is to be healed, and we know that God can renew us and move us from contention to meekness, from pride to humility. He desires for us to conform to Biblical principles and for our "hearts" (emotions) to be changed. Proverbs 17:27 relates "He that hath knowledge spareth his

121

words and a man of understanding is of an excellent spirit." Folks, that is such a promise! As we have previously stated, the Hebrew word is "yagar," which among its possible rendering is the word "cool". It doesn't quite follow teen vernacular, but it does imply that when others are upset, there is at least one person who is "refined and cool." As a result of our study, there are at least four areas where we are challenged to change.

Change Number One --- Your understanding has been opened. Let's define understanding as the "process of gaining insight." Some call this process illumination, revelation, or self-realization. In Luke 24, a resurrected Jesus confronted his disciples. They were not aware that it was Jesus. The passage relates that in verse 27, He opened to them first the Scriptures. We have attempted to do that in this material. Secondly, in verse 31, the passage relates that "their eyes were opened and they knew him ..." Hopefully, concerning your argumentative spirit, your "eyes have been opened." Verse 32 is so insightful, it relates that, "they said one to another, did not our heart burn within us?" As you anticipate this "new you" that God is building, are you excited? Is your heart burning within you? Then, finally, in verse 45 he "opened their understanding." Do you see it all differently?

I recall a lady whose four-year-old son picked up her husband's service revolver (he was a policeman), and in what he thought to be play, pointed the gun toward a two-year-old brother. The trigger was pulled, a bullet was discharged, and the child was killed instantly. She ran to the scene, picked up the child, and in total hysteria rushed from neighbor to neighbor screaming for help. The event "triggered" a delusionary state, and not only was there denial concerning the death of Danny, but also she was compulsively driven to find and locate the "anti-Christ." We could not get her admitted willingly into a hospital, because the admitting psychiatrist could not "pass" her "religious examination." My first three counseling sessions with this lady were Bible studies on eschatology (doctrine of end times). She would bring "reams" of notes and stacks of books to our sessions. She would talk incessantly. During the fourth session, she came in subdued. There were no notes or books. I looked at her said; "Danny is dead, isn't he?"

She looked up somewhat puzzled and retorted, "Yes, Danny is dead." She then cried hysterically. The crying must have continued for two minutes. I held her and the tears flowed onto my shirt. At this point, the actual therapy was initiated, and she became an excellent patient.

Watchman Nee refers to this process as intuition. He believes that intuition is the sensing organ of the spirit. His defense includes verses such as Mark 2:8, where Jesus, " ... perceived in his spirit ..." The thought is a bit fascinating. Is it not? The notion of a sensing process within the human spirit has many ramifications. He relates in his book, *The Spiritual Man*. "...it is through the intuition part of the spirit that we are able to distinguish what is from God and what is not ... there is only one kind of truth that is valuable concerning God and that is the truth that is revealed in our spirit by God's Spirit." We sense the need for change, and "intuition" is used of God to initiate this process.

Moving this process from "intuition" to "rational consciousness" is experiencing understanding. We can understand the argumentative spirit.

Change Number two --- Communication skills are changing. Before us now is the challenge of conforming our spirit and soul to Biblical principles. How should our journey, thus far, change our communication skills? If our argumentative spirit has been healed, how are we different? Let's consider four possibilities. Now, understand there are "hundreds" more.

(1) *Learn to say it and be quiet.* Matthew 5:37 states, "Let your communication be yes, yes, and no, no, and whatsoever is more than this comes from the evil one." We have commented how the continuation of an argument is of the devil, and how difficult is it to have the self-control to express our opinions and be quiet? I recall hearing a lady disciplining her children with this phrase, "What part of no do you not understand?" She had made clear to her child that he was not "getting his way", and now she was closing the discussion. I must confess, it was never easy for me to "walk away". I had to have the last word ... and the last word ... and the last word. I love the passage in Proverbs 16:23 which states, "The heart of the wise teacheth his mouth and addeth learning to his lips." It is interesting how the heart "teaches" the mouth. Now, there is a concept. Let's quote it one more time. Proverbs 17:27 states, "He that hath knowledge sparreth his words; and a man of understanding is of an excellent spirit." Hopefully, this thought has challenged us to have more self-control.

(2) **Learn how to respond softly.** Proverbs 15:1 says, "A soft answer turns away wrath, but grievous words stir up anger." The word "grievous" is pointed and sharp. The word for soft is "weak or faint." How much would we have to change to move from saying words that are sharp and hurtful and words that are weak and faint? I recall while directing a Christian radio station, I received a call from an irate advertiser. My secretary forewarned me. "This person is upset." She was correct. Even though I directed a Christian station, obviously, all of our advertisers were not religious people. When I lifted the phone, he began, "Let me tell you …" and in no uncertain terms he did... Frankly, some of his points were exaggerated, but some points were well taken. His comments were sharp and grievous. It is amazing what Biblical principle can do. My "wounded" spirit felt retort, and my "hurting" soul said rebuttal, but the Lord was laying the foundation for these words that you are reading. Believe it or not, I thought of this Biblical principle. "He must eventually stop," I thought. When he did, the first thing from my mouth was, "I am sorry, will you forgive us? Tell me please what I can do to make it right." Immediately, the tone of his voice went down, and we were able to amicably work through a context of resolve. This principle can change the tone of your voice.

(3) **Learn to edify others with your words.** There are two strong passages to share at this point. Romans 15:1-2 states, "We then that are strong ought to bear the infirmities of the weak, and not to please ourselves. Let everyone of us please his neighbor for his good to edification." Ephesians 4:29, "Let no corrupt (or

needless) communication proceed out of your mouth, but that which is good to the use of edifying that it may administer grace to the hearers." The word for edifies means to "build-up." Through words, we have the ability to "build up" others. There is a pretense that the strong will bear the infirmities of the weak. And imagine, through our words we have the ability to administer grace (or God's favor) to others.

As our children were being raised, we seldom went to movies. Part of this was principle and part of this was money. I do recall taking my family to see that "spine thriller" called Bambi. In the movie, there was a little rabbit called "thumper." He was called "thumper", because every time he did something wrong, he would bow his head and his foot would start moving up and down. I fell in love with him immediately. I guess I identified somewhat with him and his mischievous spirit. Well in the movie, he was making derogatory comments about Bambi, and his mother disciplined him with the remarks, "What did your father tell you?" He bowed his head (with his foot moving up and down) and said, "If you can't say something good about someone, say nothing at all." Well ... after the movie. I said to my kids in the car. "Let's learn from Thumper. From now on if I hear you talk about others, I will simply say Thumper, and hopefully, you will remember his principle." I think my kids came to dislike rabbits in general and Thumper in particular.

And this principle you can put to practice immediately. No matter where you are at work, or at church, or at school, you can always say something nice to people. How much effort does it take to say, "You look nice today, I always appreciate your smile?" That's it ... right now, put the book down and tell your spouse, your kids ... how wonderful they are and how much you love them.

(4) **Learn to be sensitive to communication cues.** Philippians 2:3-4 challenges us to "let nothing be done through strife or vainglory, but in lowliness of mind let each esteem other better than themselves. Look not every man on his own things, but every man also on the things of others." The number one criterion of mental health is the ability to put others before ourselves. As others are talking, are we thinking of them or, are we thinking of ourselves? Do we esteem others better than ourselves? Do we want to talk about us, or do we talk about them? One thing we know....if we choose our words well, people always like to talk about themselves.

If my wife says, "Boy, I have had a hard day", do I not have many alternative responses? I can say "Doing what (ouch)?" Probably then I should back up and wait for some fire. I can say, "You think you have had a hard day, let me tell you about my day." Or I can say, "I understand, I love you." She is crying for "help." Am I listening? If the house was on fire, I would probably respond quickly. Do we listen for communication cues?

Change Number Three ---The soul and body have been broken. Watchman Nee refers to this process as the "breaking of the outer man." I call it "the modification of the will." Why have you had the particular circumstances of your life? Why has your life had so much stress and tension? Is it possible that you have "misread" God's purpose in all of this? Watchman Nee suggested that there must be an "annihilation" of the soul and body. When we go through this "breaking" process, circumstances are perceived differently. From his book, *The Release of the Spirit*, he relates, "Our spirit is given to us by God to enable us to respond to Him. But the outward man is ever responding to things without, hence depriving us from the presence of God. We cannot destroy all the things without, but we can break down the outward man. If, through the mercy of God, our outward man is broken, we may be characterized as the following: yesterday, we were full of curiosity, but today it is impossible to be curious. Formerly, our emotions could be easily aroused, either stirring our love, the most delicate emotion or provoking our temper, the crudest of them. But no matter how many things crowd upon us, now our inward man remains unmoved; the presence of God is changed, and our inner peace is unruffled. It becomes evident that the breaking of the outward man is the basis for enjoying God's presence".

I perceive this as a will modification process. Scriptures make clear that Moses' will was broken before he was used. Paul had a light come from heaven and knock him to the ground. A voice came from heaven and said, "Saul, Saul, why persecutest thou me?" When Paul became convinced that this was God speaking directly to him, he dramatically changed. Peter is my favorite. He vowed during the events of Calvary that he would remain faithful. Jesus related that he would deny him three times. He not only denied him, but he then went off and wept. Let's remember that it was Peter who led the first church in Jerusalem. This "will modification" process was part of his schooling.

I know that to some, this process can be devastating, and sometimes God's purposes are difficult to understand. But He wants our will. I think of Joni Erikson Tadas. She was paralyzed as a teenager, and she has spent her life in a wheelchair, but God had a special touch and a special ministry for her. Many years ago, I had the privilege of "interviewing" her on radio. As we were discussing the victories and traumas of her life, I asked "in the flow" what might seem to some a ridiculous question. I said, "Joni, do you consider yourself handicapped?" I will never forget her answer. She replied, "Not anymore." It is safe to assume that she had moved through this process.

Change Number Four --- The Inner Man has been released. God desires to heal us. Hebrews 12:12-13, "Wherefore lift up the hands which hang down, and the feeble knees. And make straight paths for your feet, lest that which is lame be turned out of the way, but let it rather be healed". And note that after the healing we are admonished to "follow peace with all men..." Can we imagine a world where the human spirits "universally" are healed? Can we imagine a world where the first responses of our spirit and soul are not to hate, or to be angry, or to kill, but our first response is one of peace? Let's start striving for a healing of our spirit, and hope, that this truth can become universal. So many of us are carrying wounds from the past. Tragically for some, Satan has gotten a "foothold" in our lives, and through his distortion and perversion, the healing process has become more difficult. Let's stop for a minute and ask the Lord for a healing. Please pray with me.

> "*Dear Father, I am so tired of caring the baggage from my life. I know that I have been in bondage, but dear Father I want to be released. Forgive me for violating your principles and living within my own flesh. I want to pray specifically for my sin of an argumentative spirit and also for (any others)_____ Dear Father, in Jesus' name I acknowledge the working of the Holy Spirit within me and your desire to change me, and I know you want to free me. I pray for a healing now, and I thank you for it. In Jesus' name.*"

To Watchman Nee, few Christians ever experience the "release of the spirit." Nee challenged, "There is an immutable law of God's working in us; His specific purpose is breaking us and releasing our spirit for free exercise ... whatever the things to which you are bound, God will deal with them one after another. Not even such trivialities as clothing, eating, or drinking will escape the careful hand of the Holy Spirit. Until the day comes when all these are destroyed, you will not know perfect liberty.

I suppose every church has at least one Aunt Bertha. What makes Aunt Bertha so special is that she is not preoccupied with herself. You observe her busy loving people. She cooks for the suppers. She always compassionately prays for others. It is not unusual for her to be a "hugger." And somehow her love for people has "blinded" her to others' faults. Some within the church might say that she is naive. Let's just be "thankful" that we don't have a whole church of Aunt Berthas. Can you imagine? Can you imagine a whole block full of Aunt Berthas, or a city, or a country, or a world? It has to start with people like you and me

Ezekiel 18:31 exhorts us to "rid yourselves of all offenses you have committed, and get a new heart and a new spirit." II Corinthians 7:1 states, "Having therefore these promises, dearly beloved, let us cleanse ourselves from all filthiness of the flesh and spirit, perfecting holiness in the fear of the Lord." Ephesians 4:30-32 states that we should not, "grieve the Holy Spirit of God, whereby ye are sealed unto the day of redemption. Let all bitterness, and wrath, and anger, and clamor and evil speaking be put away from you with all malice. And be ye kind one to another, tenderhearted, forgiving one another, even as God for Christ's sake hath forgiven you."

Watchman Nee cautions us that the "release of the spirit" cannot happen "artificially." I believe his thought is that ultimately God must do it for us. James 4:8 admonishes us that if we "draw nigh to God ... he will draw nigh to (us)." This is so true. The healing of the spirit cannot happen by taking pills or doing exercises, or we would all do it. It does start, however, I contend with a "contrite spirit" with a "hunger and thirst after righteousness." And we do have the promise that if we have that hunger, God will fill us (Matthew 5:6).

This epilogue. Thank you for taking this journey with me. This has been both an academic and spiritual trip for me. I certainly need to thank my wife and family for their tolerance and forgiveness. But it is interesting ... through the stresses of marriage, life, and raising children, I was forced to gain insights into all of these areas and into myself. The Scriptures relate that "in everything" we should give thanks; so I am thankful for a rough environmental childhood, and I am thankful for a "strong willed" father, and I am thankful for the three times that I have been close to death, especially the car accidents, and I am thankful for all my stresses. Interestingly, Psalm 139:12-16 relates, "my days were numbered when I was in my mother's womb. Such an awesome God... Ephesians 1:11 states that, "all things happen after the counsel of his will." I contend that the most profound thought that we can think is how the Lord goes before us. If you made it to this last thought, God must have "numbered your days" also. Blessings.

Also from Baal Hamon Publishers:

Worship That Pleases God - by James W. Bartley, Jr. (PhD)
February 2008, 360 pages, 6' x 9'
ISBN 9780756884 (Paperback: US $17.99, UK £13.99)
Category: Non-fiction

James W. Bartley Jr. has gone beyond the common status quo to explore a subject that most authors do not have sufficient experiential credentials to delve into. He practically reflects on his more than 60 years experience of walking with God to bring many

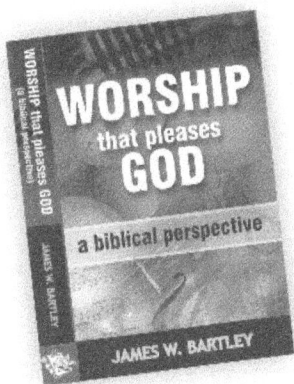

into an awe-striking deeper communion with God. His book, Worship that pleases God gives an accurate insight into the inexhaustible subject of Worship – as an invaluable asset in the Man-God relationship. Being a retired Professor of theology, Dr. Bartley has successfully made a holistic and unassailable exposition of worship – as a theme that finds its root in the book of Genesis and continues to Revelation in the Bible, while his academic perception lends credence to his work. Worship that pleases God is not just a book that enriches the knowledge of inquisitive readers; Dr. Bartley has carefully sequenced it in such a manner that even the least motivated reader will simply find the wave of his discovered supernatural worship pattern so irresistible.

Also from Baal Hamon Publishers:

The Fatherless – a novel by Erin Inman
February 2008, 420 pages, 5.5' x 8.5'
ISBN 9780756914 (Paperback: US $17.99, UK £13.99)
Category: Fiction

Nick Pierce, a talented young boy whose singular obsession is music, finds himself overturned from a lonely life with his grandmother in Wichita, Kansas to the rather strange atmosphere of life in Western Kansas with the father he had never met. Although a friendly neighbor couple takes Nick under their wing, circumstances in life and his father's attitude work against him. In search for a way to fulfill his uttermost desires, he enters into a world of the unknown – a stranger world that leads him into questioning right from wrong. In the face of a life-threatening sickness, Nick wonders if life could offer him a little more, if music may still flow from his fingers, in praise to the Father-God.

Order from www.baalhamon.com

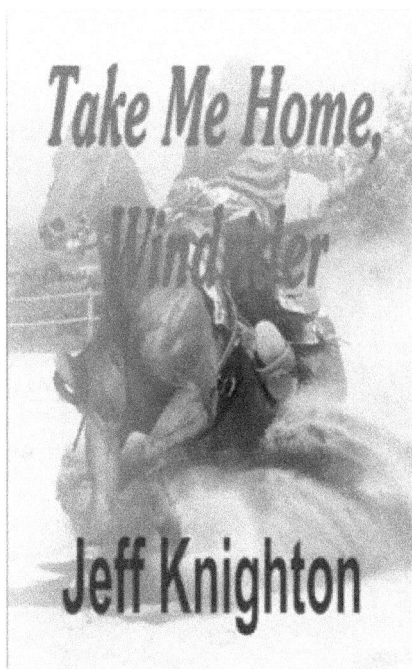

Also from Baal Hamon Publishers:

Does God Truly Exist? – by Temitope Oyetomi
August 2006, 360 pages, 6' x 9'
ISBN 9780756825 (Paperback: US $17.99)
Category: Non-fiction

Archbishop Akinola, Primate of the Church of Nigeria (Anglican Communion) 2000 – 2010, commends this book as a "valuable material for anyone tired of dodging the questions". Indeed, it is one book that has "raised a fathom of questions", as yet another Bishop - a PhD-holder - observes in the foreword. However, the tact with which the author resolves many of these questions is scholarly and engaging. The author writes with confidence and his arguments are intelligent and highly persuasive: facts and their interpretations are presented in a style that is approachable, digestible and amenable to reading by a wide audience. Ordinarily, one might think of it as a book for those who are in doubt of God's existence. Of course, it is. But it will be more applicable to those who are sure that God exists and who believe they are worshiping the true and living God. "Who really is the true and living God" and "how best can one relate with God" are the ultimate quests of the book. Drawing answers from science, religion and philosophy, the author has contrived a rare blend "that will plausibly challenge every mind". No wonder a Baptist minister recommends it "to all people no matter their religious persuasions". It is certainly an intellectual masterpiece.

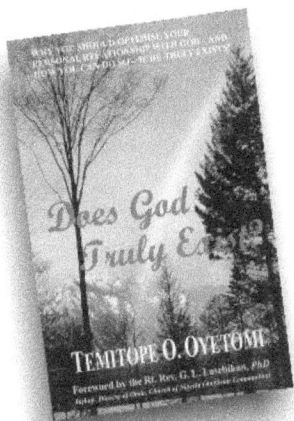

Also from Baal Hamon Publishers:

Fellow Nigerians, I Wish You Good Luck – by Temitope Oyetomi
March 2011, 160 pages, 5' x 8'
ISBN 9784956519 (Paperback: US $7.99)
Category: Non-fiction

Is there a real connection between cleverness, good governance and good luck? The answer may not be so simple and direct. That is why the author of this book an experienced editor has painstakingly ploughed through anecdotes, news, history, and reasoning to blend a masterful piece that manages to be funny, witty, pragmatic and eye-opening all at once. The primary foci of the book are issues relating to the 2011 presidential elections in Nigeria but the book goes on to open up a typical Nigerian soul in an uncommonly down-to-earth manner.

Nigeria is Africa s most populous country, often touted as the Giant of Africa and Heart of Africa . The incumbent president goes by the first name Goodluck a name which has seemingly always put him in the right places at the right times over the years. Would the Nigerian nation be electing a harbinger of good fortunes if they elect him as president in 2011? This crazy book broaches on that sensitive question whilst dwelling more on extant issues that perennially afflict the Heart of Africa and relentlessly taunt the Giant of Africa.

More About Dr. Cuthbertson's Ministry:

In the mind of the Lord, Growing Together Ministries was founded to impact hurting individuals, marriages and families by providing a source of renewal and restoration for their faith in God.

Growing Together Ministries began in 1970. Dr. Duane Cuthbertson had been working with Personality Dynamics (a Christian Counseling center) in Ann Arbor, MI. He observed a woman "turned away" for counseling because she lacked hospitalization. Dr. Cuthbertson offered to counsel her and her husband "free" at a local church and the counseling portion of Growing Together Ministries was born. Since then, Duane has counseled hundreds of individuals and couples for no charge.

While working for Personality Dynamics, Dr. Cuthbertson was also serving as the Assistant Pastor at Grace Bible Church (also in Ann Arbor). The Pastor, Dr. Raymond Saxe, started an evening Bible study in which Duane taught a class on marriage. This birthed the Christian seminar portion of Growing Together Ministries. Since that time, Duane has addressed more than 100,000 people working with such organizations as ACSI (Association of Christian Schools International), ICEA (International Christian School Association), Moody College and numerous other Bible conferences and denominations. He now travels to local churches and presents seminars in such areas as marriage and Biblical child rearing.

Dr. Cuthbertson married his high school sweetheart, and at last count their five children have presented them with eighteen grandchildren.

Visit **www.growingtogetherministries.org** for more details.

www.ingramcontent.com/pod-product-compliance
Lightning Source LLC
Chambersburg PA
CBHW032000040426
42448CB00006B/439

9789784956574